I0392630

Kawaii Halloween

By Mindful Coloring Books

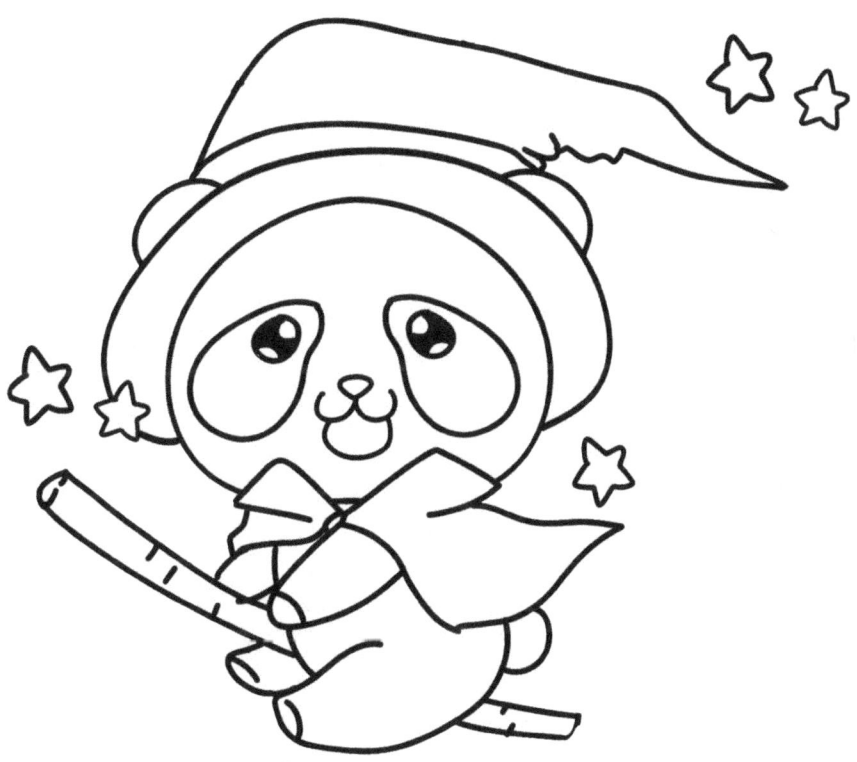

Coloring Tips

~ Sometimes what you think the color will look like and what it will actually look like are very different. Use the color test page.

~ Don't press too hard. Start out coloring lightly and you can always go back and make it darker.

~ Keep your pencil tips sharp so you can get into all the intricate spaces.

~ Using markers? Place a scrap piece of paper behind the page you are coloring. Pages in this book are only printed on one side but there is still the risk of bleed through to the next page.

~ Try different coloring utensils marketed for adults. It is fun and quality can vary greatly.

COLOR TEST PAGE

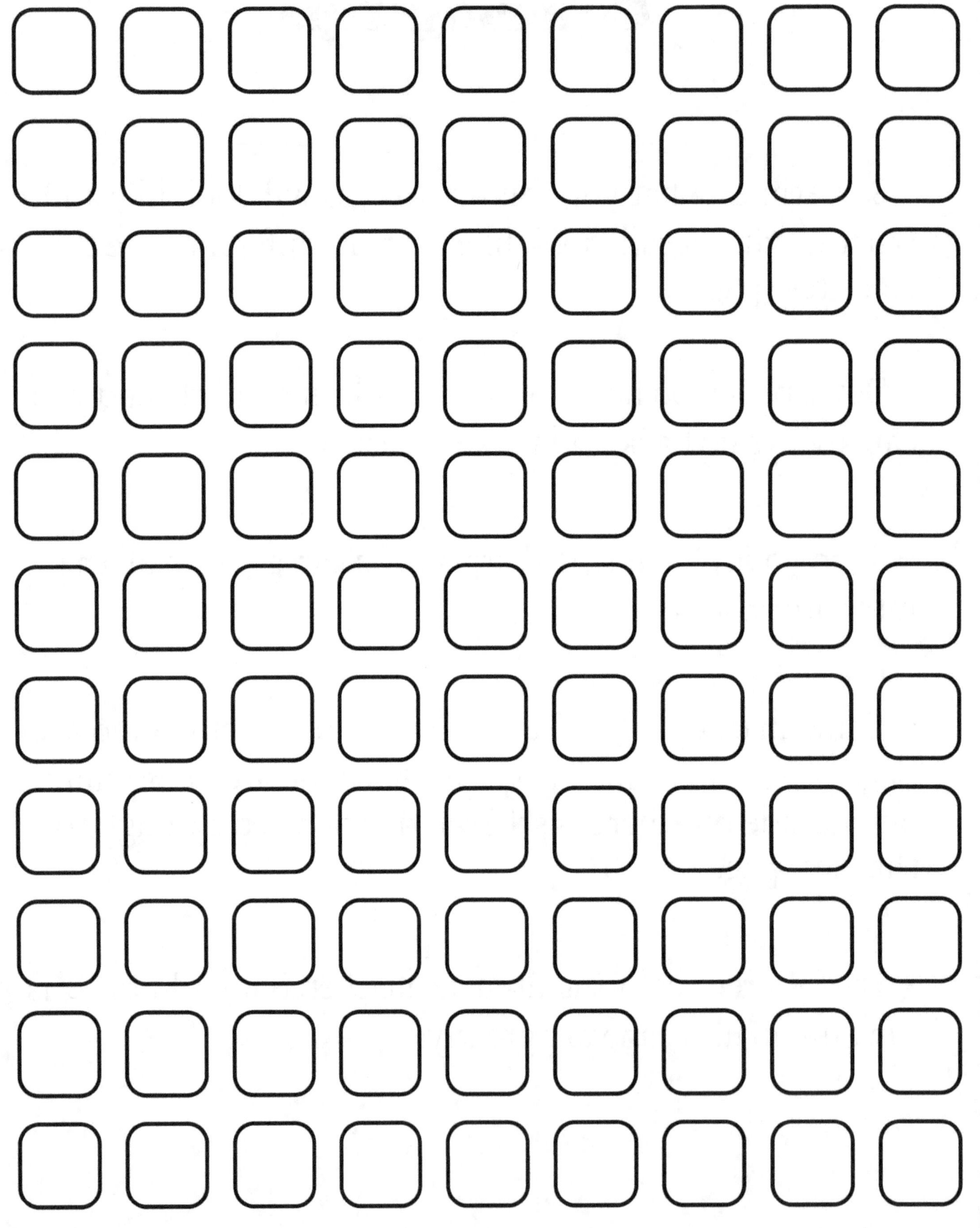

COLOR TEST PAGE

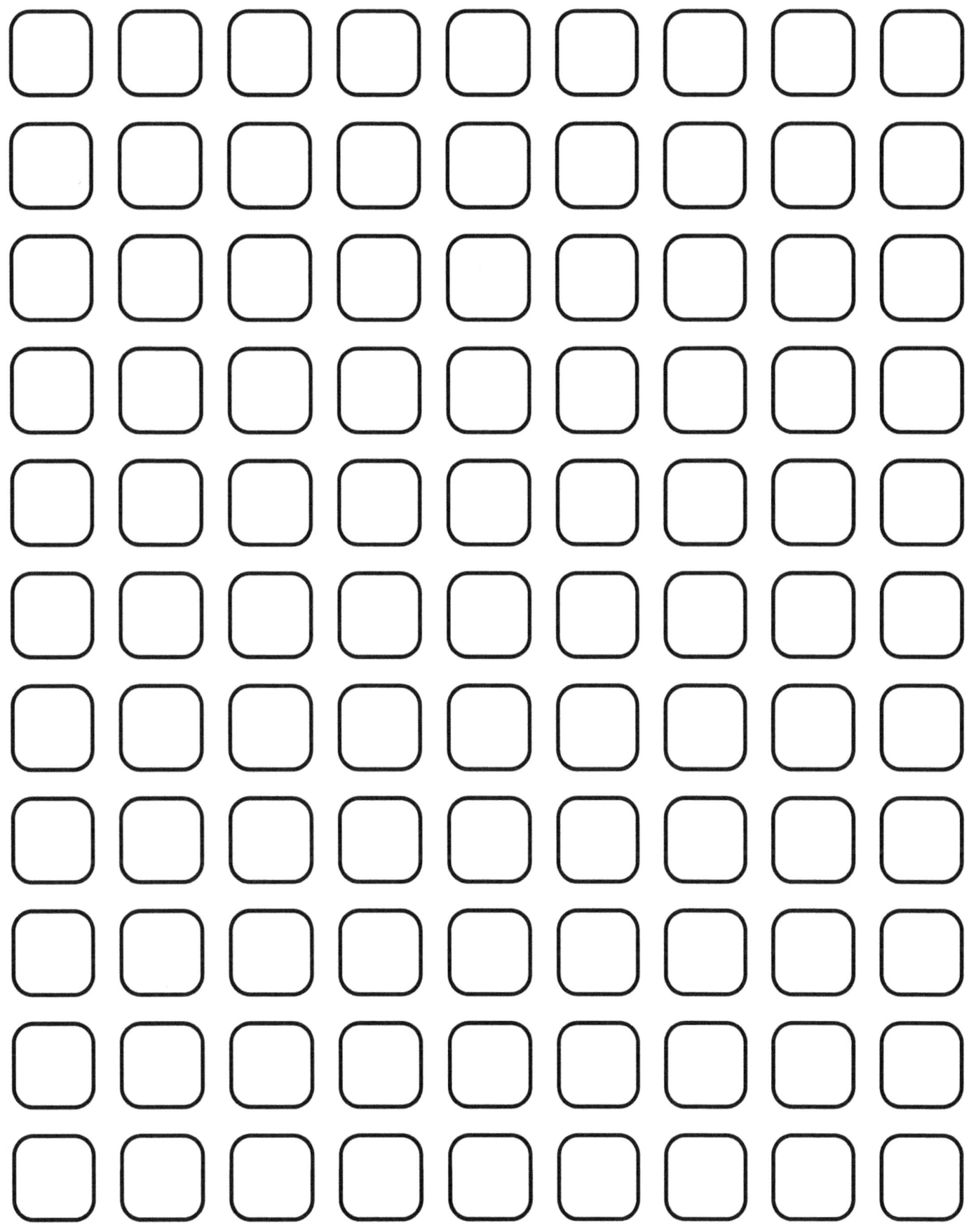

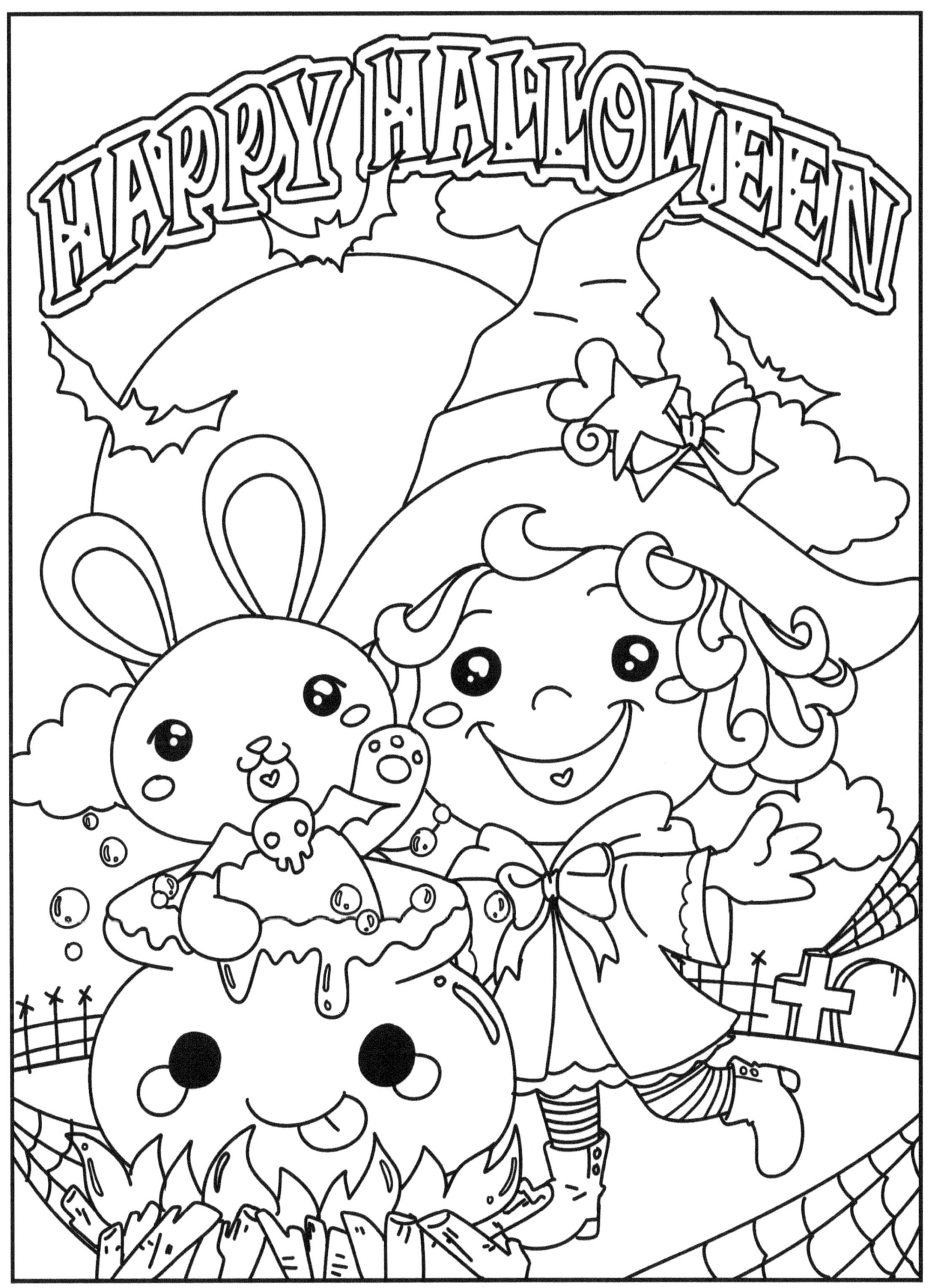

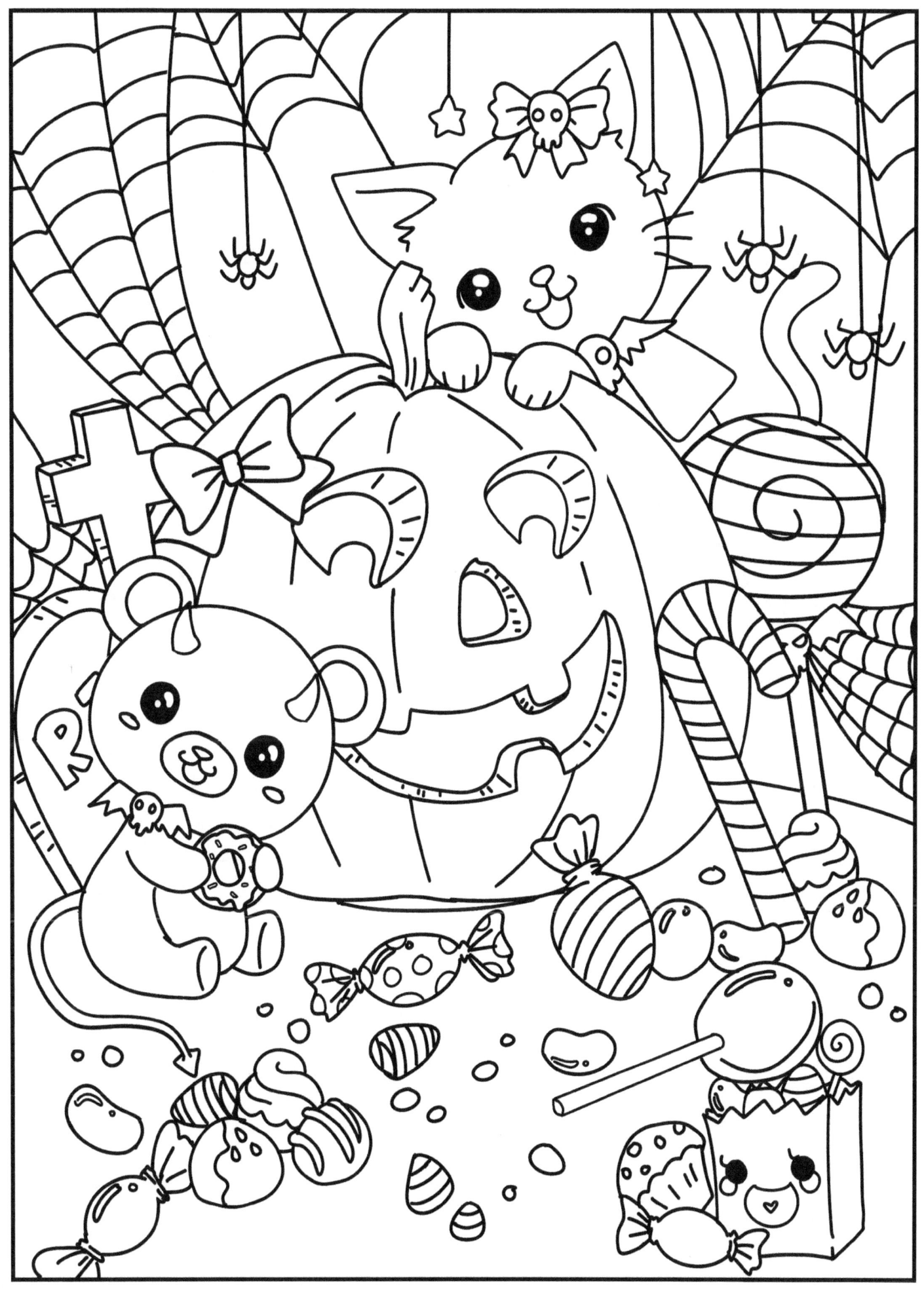

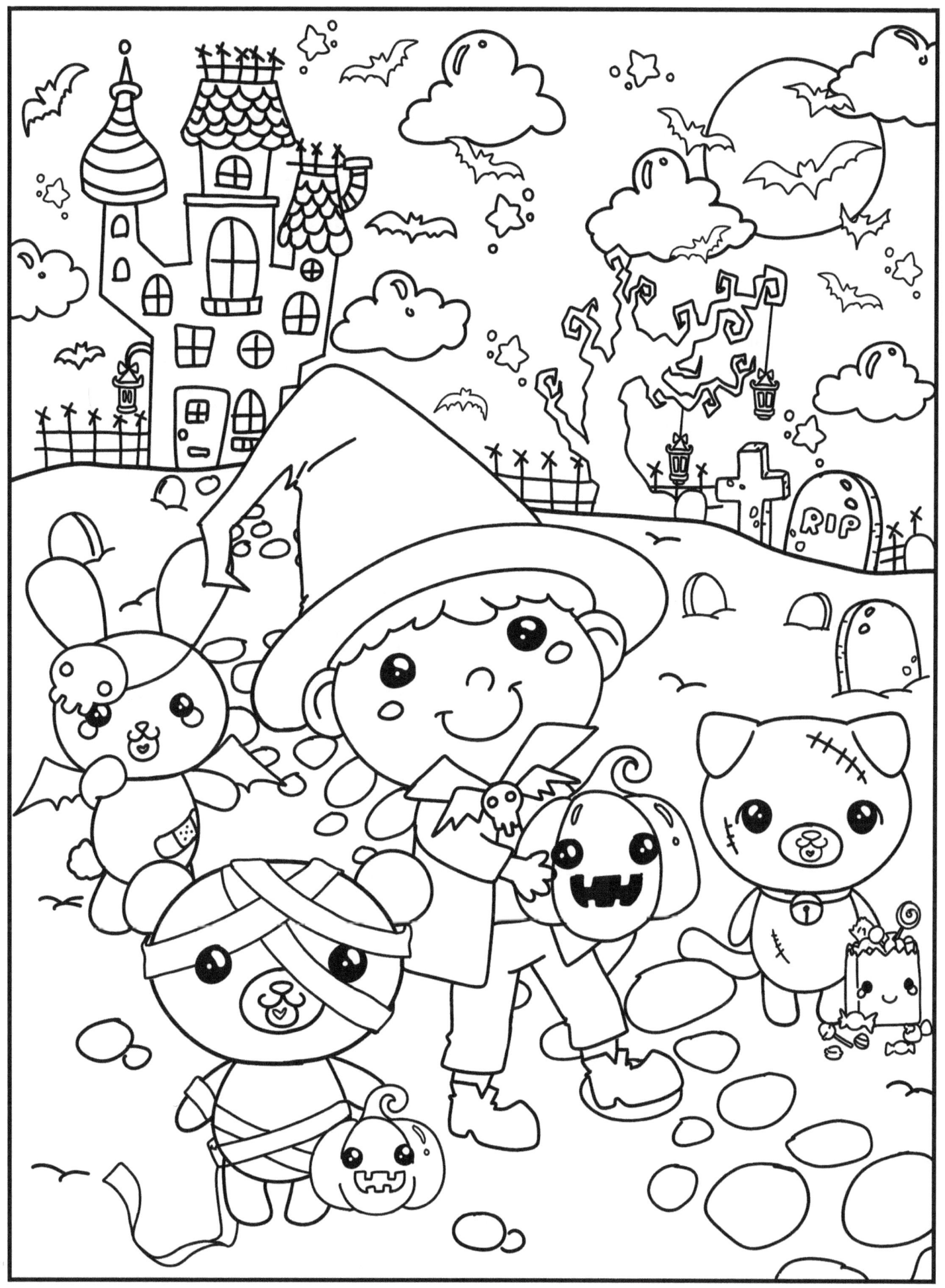

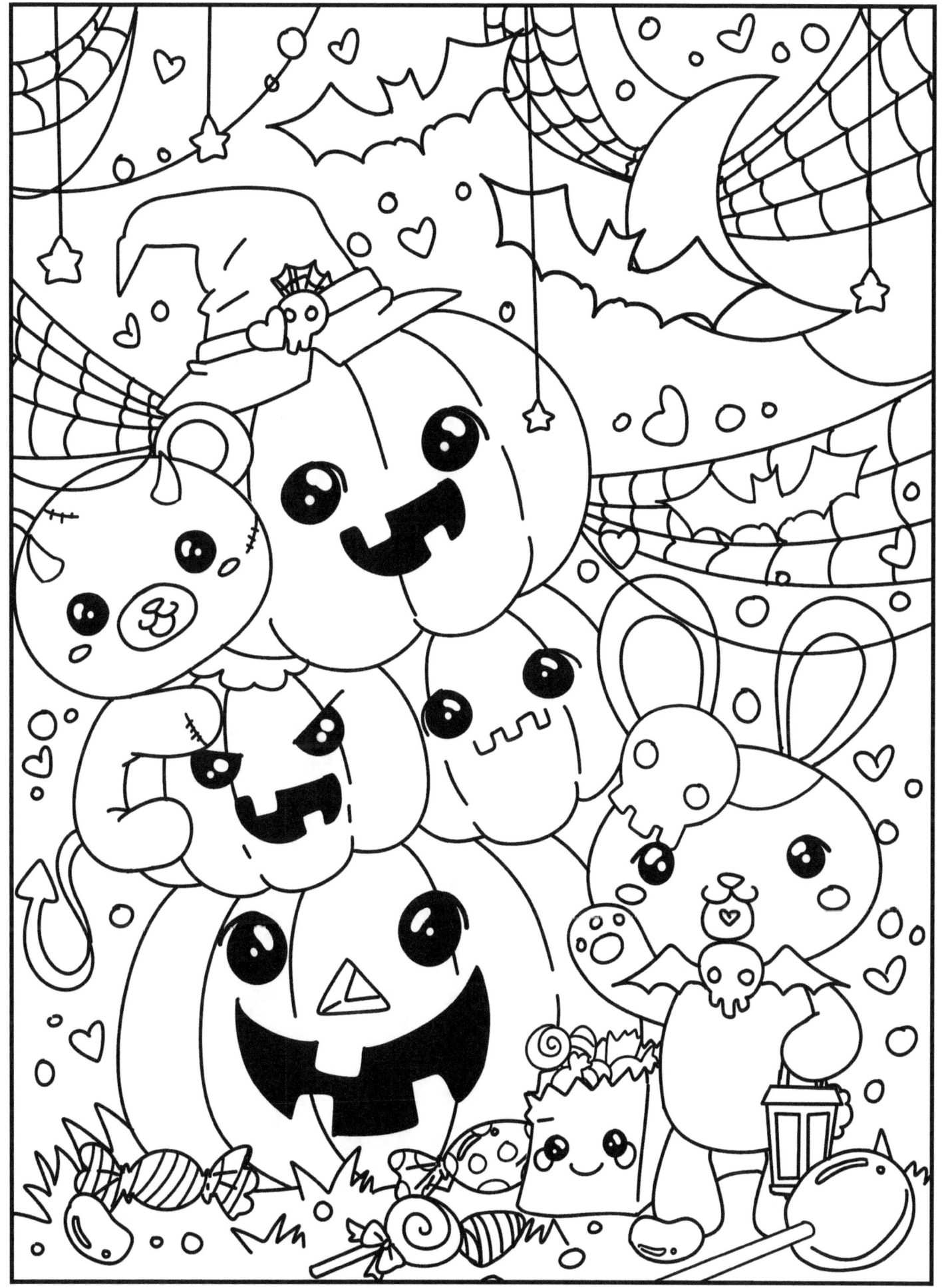

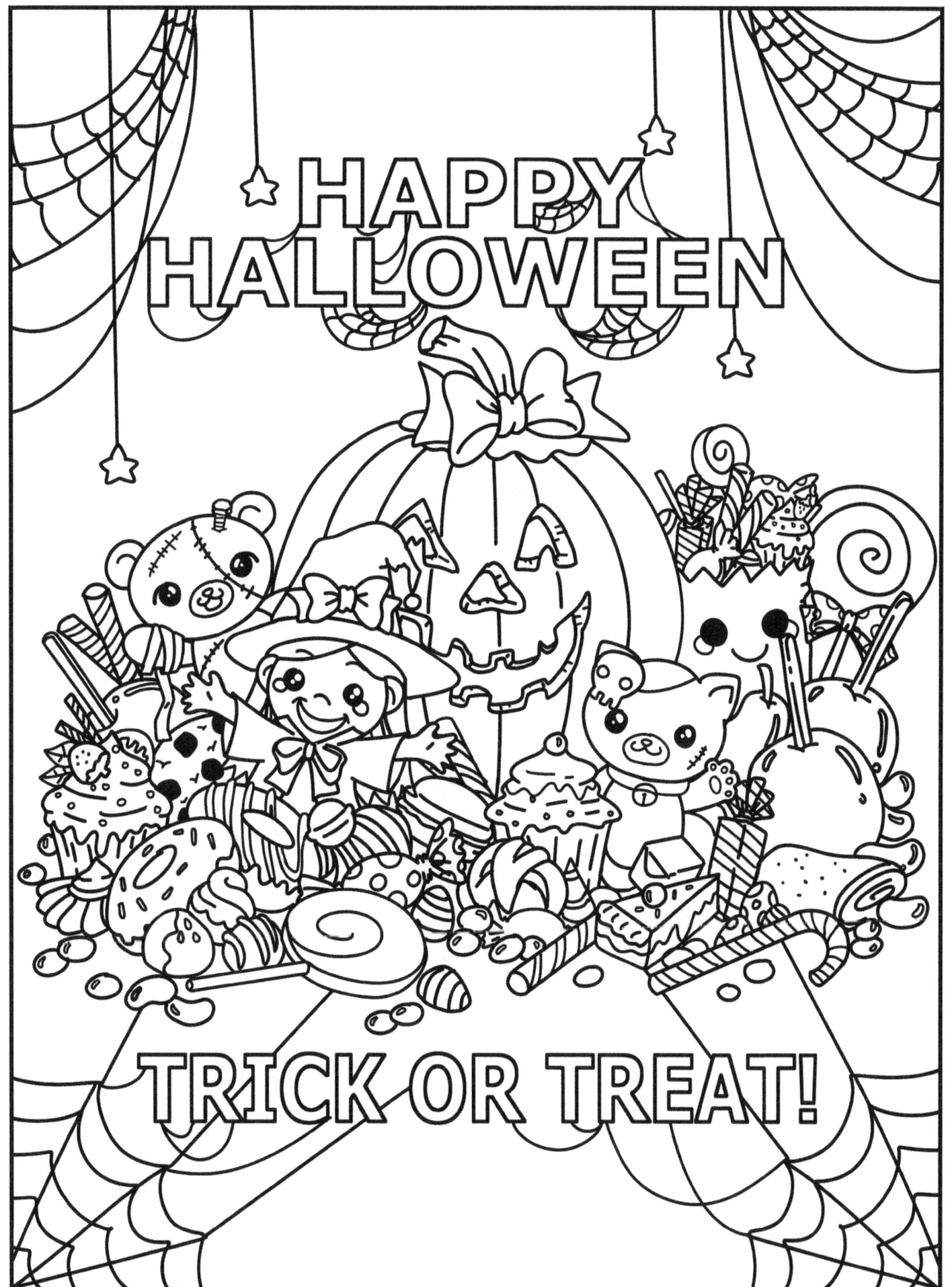

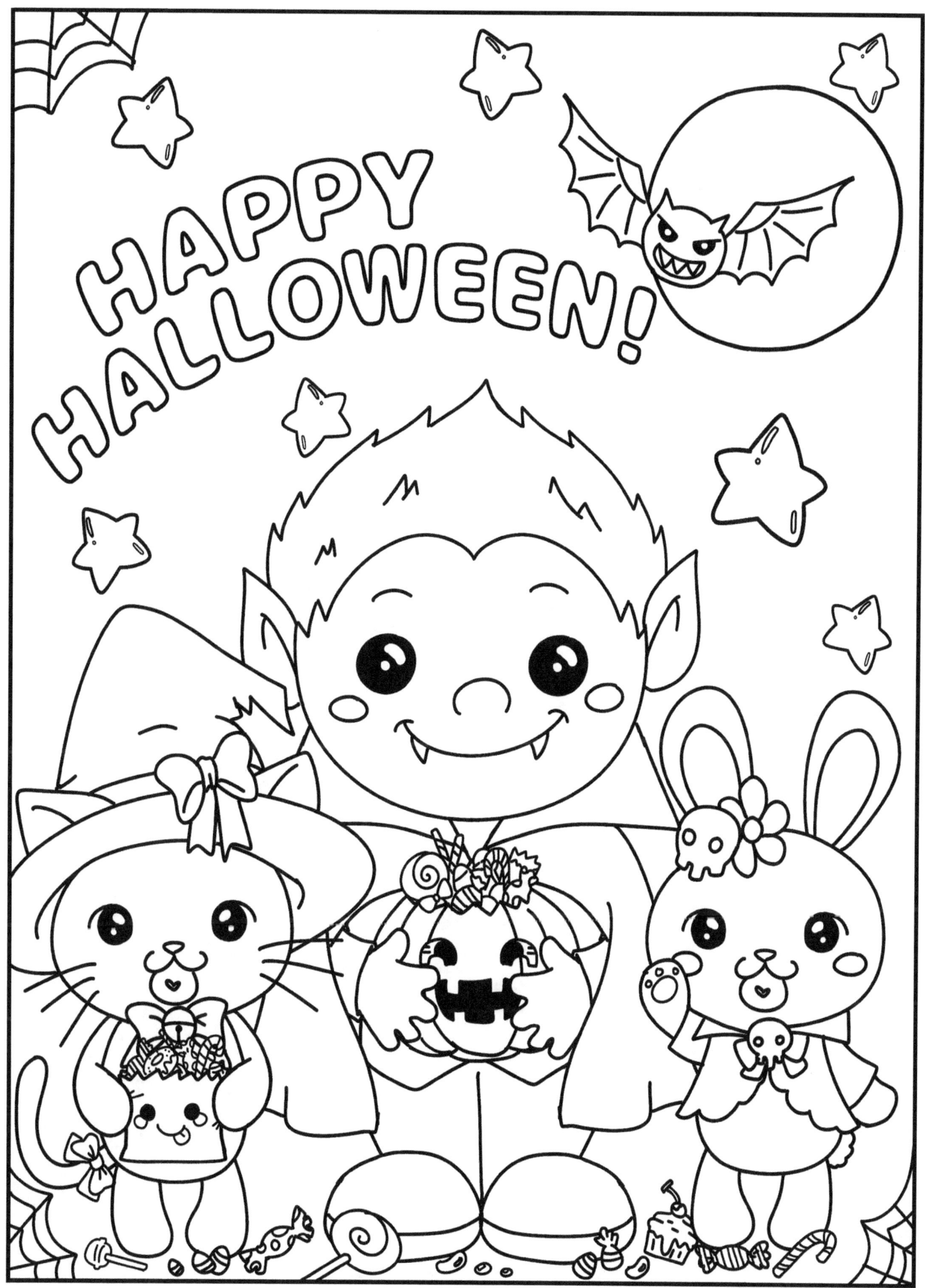

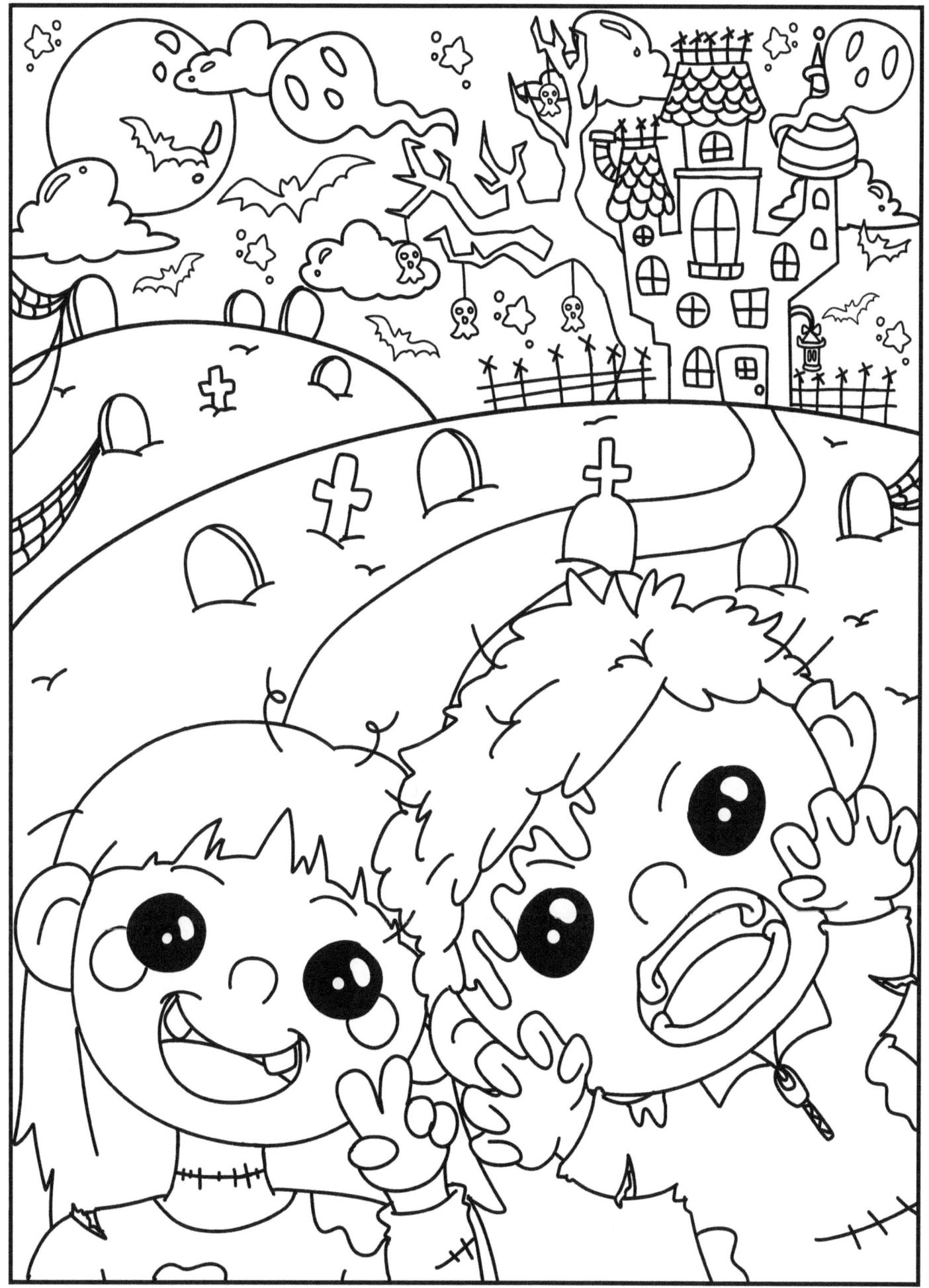

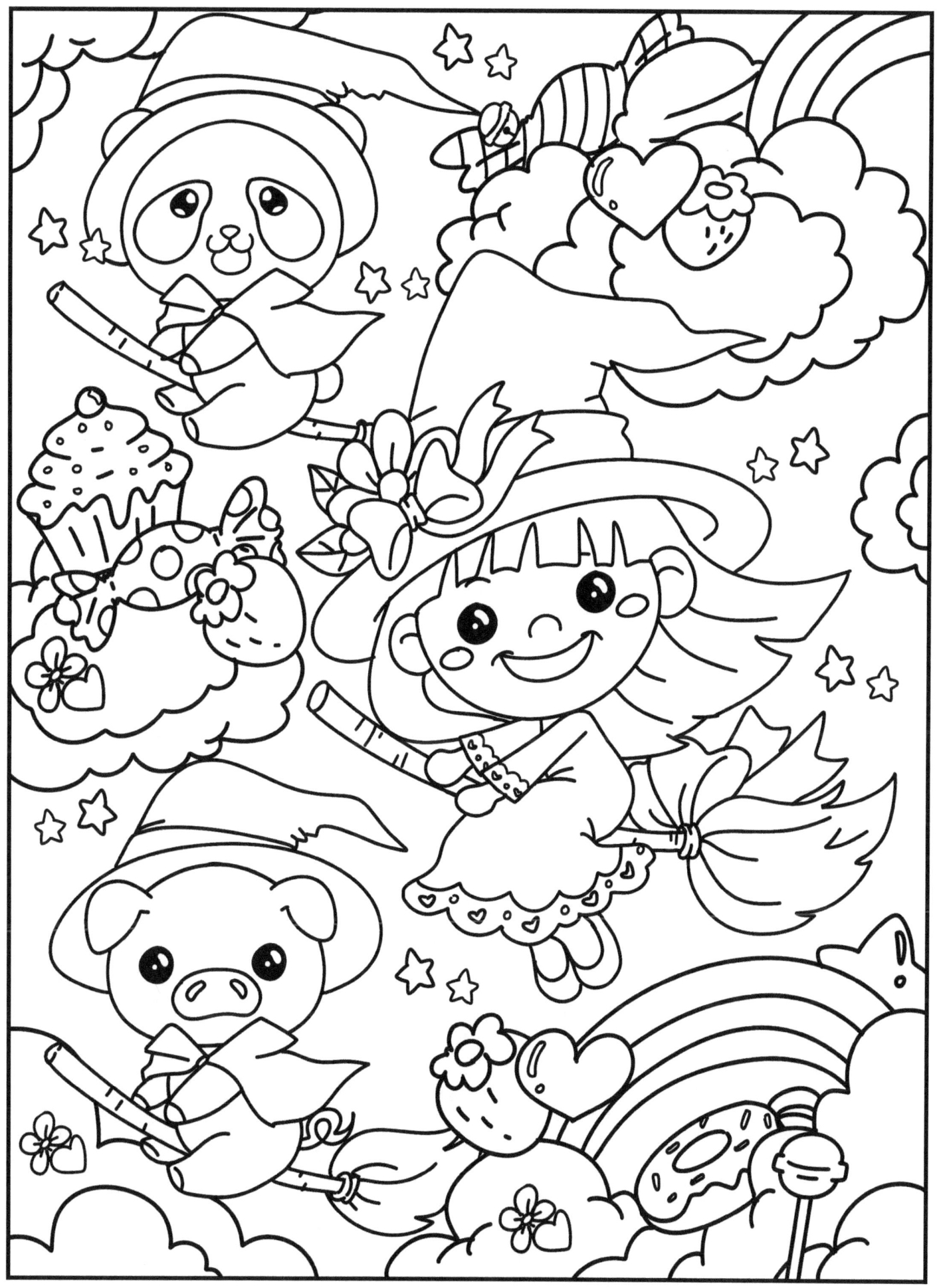

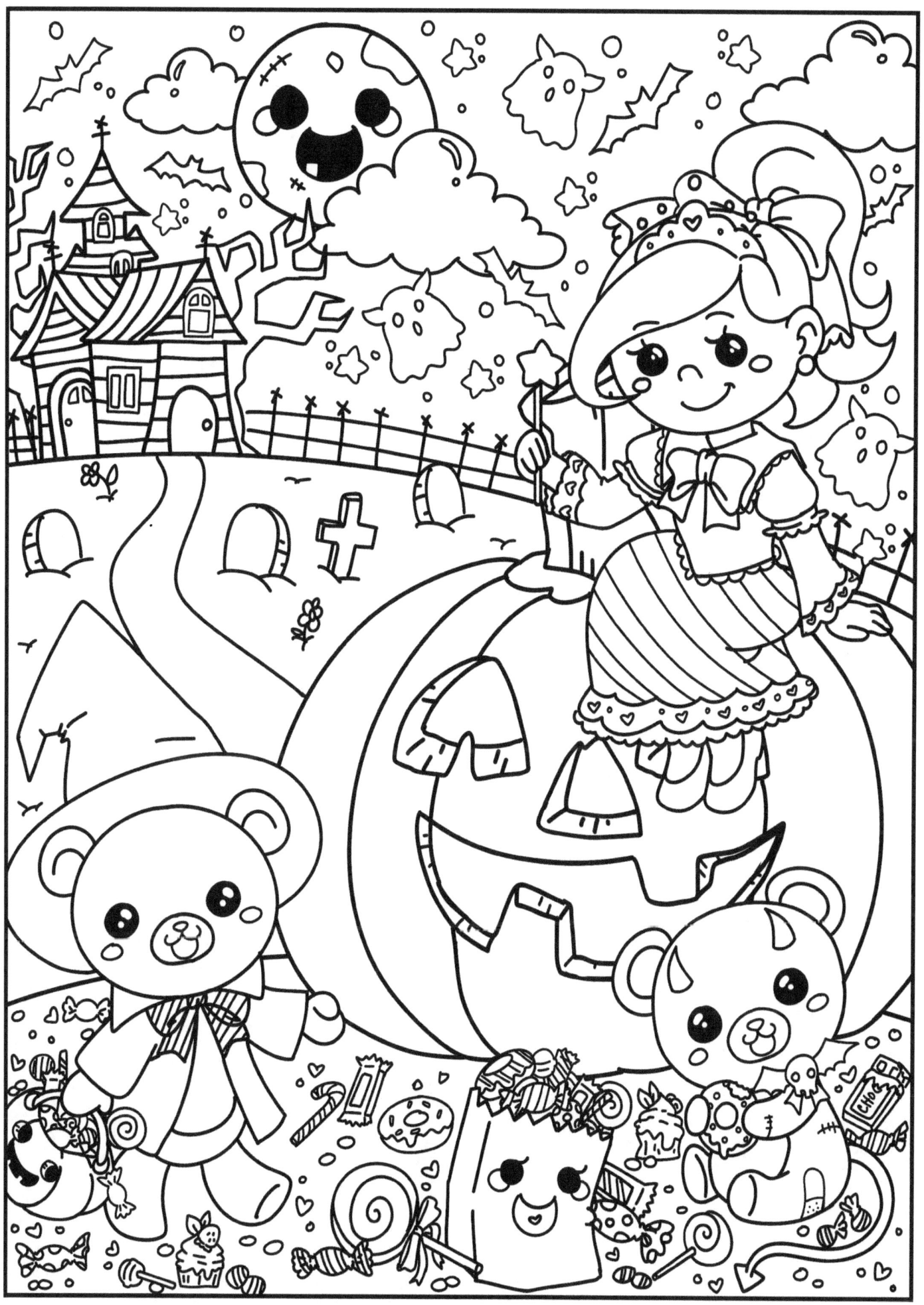

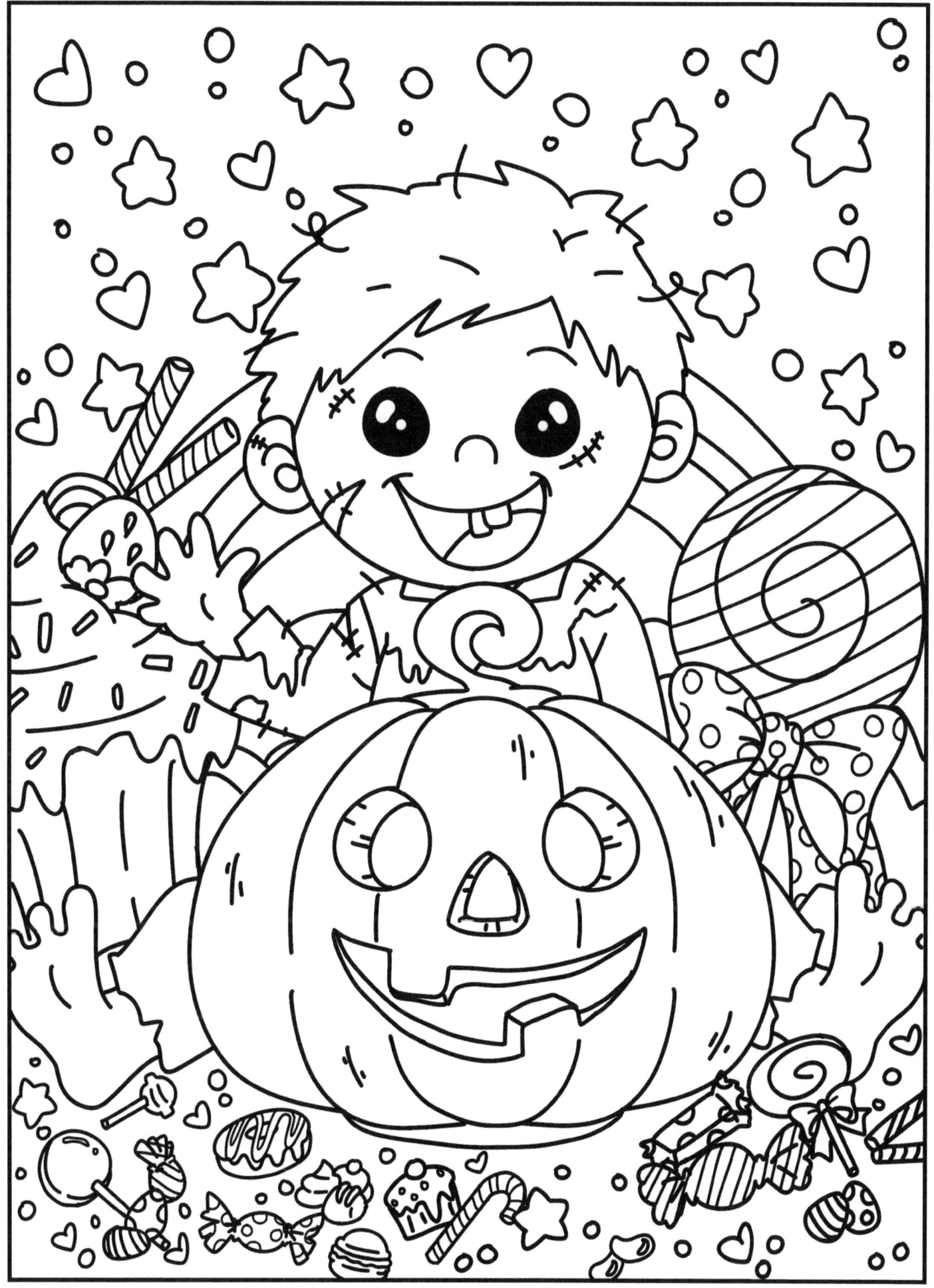

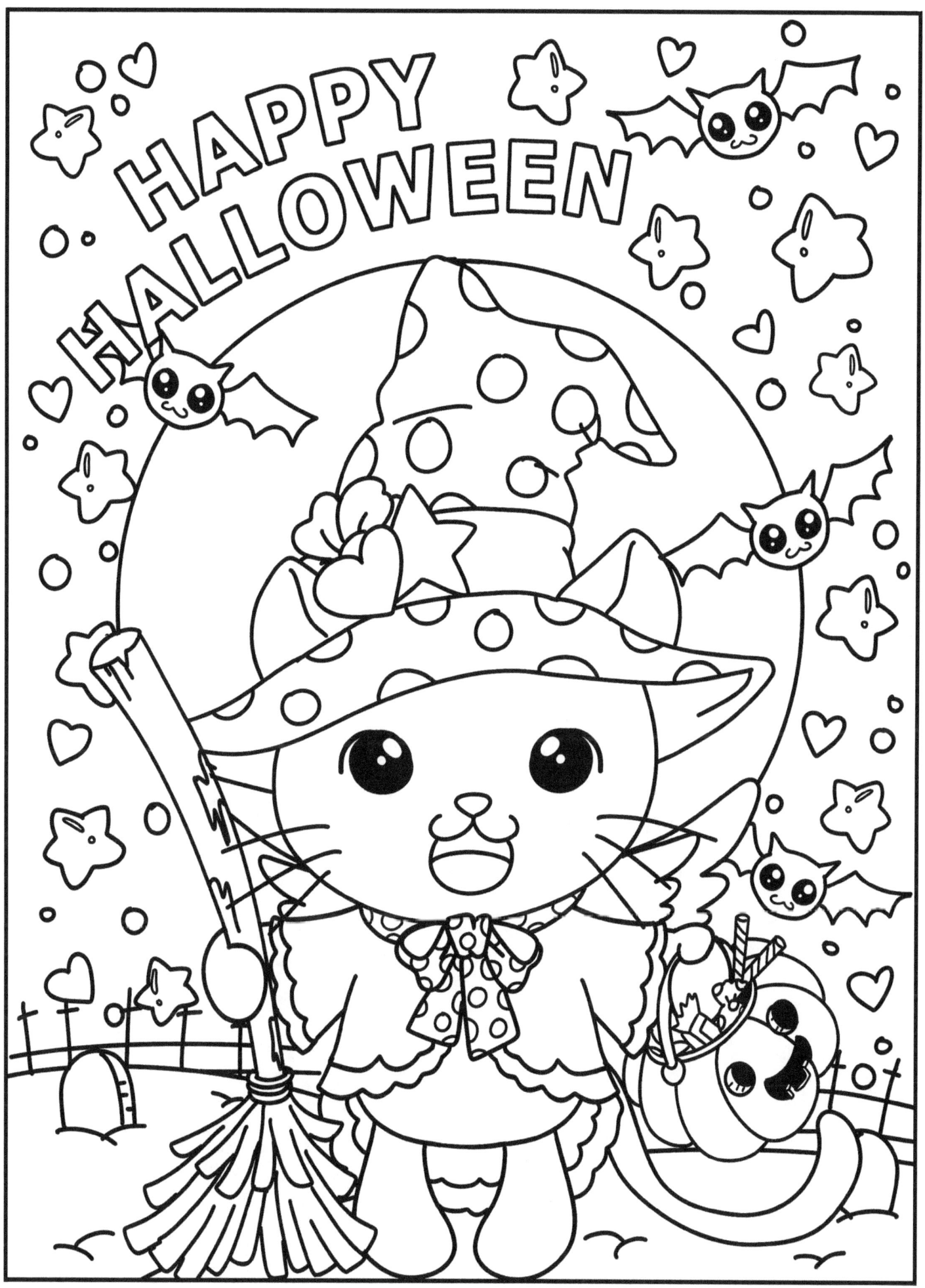

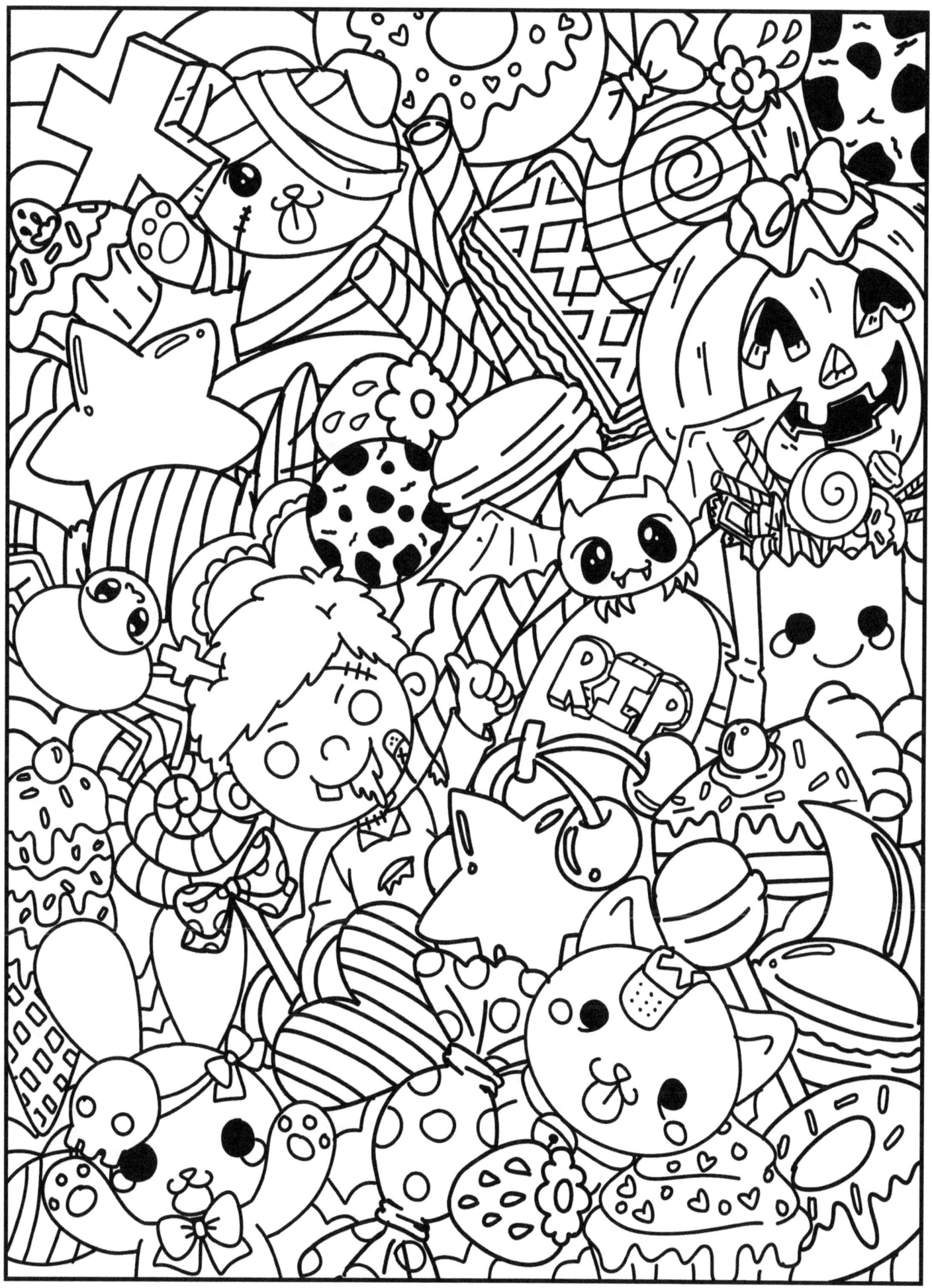

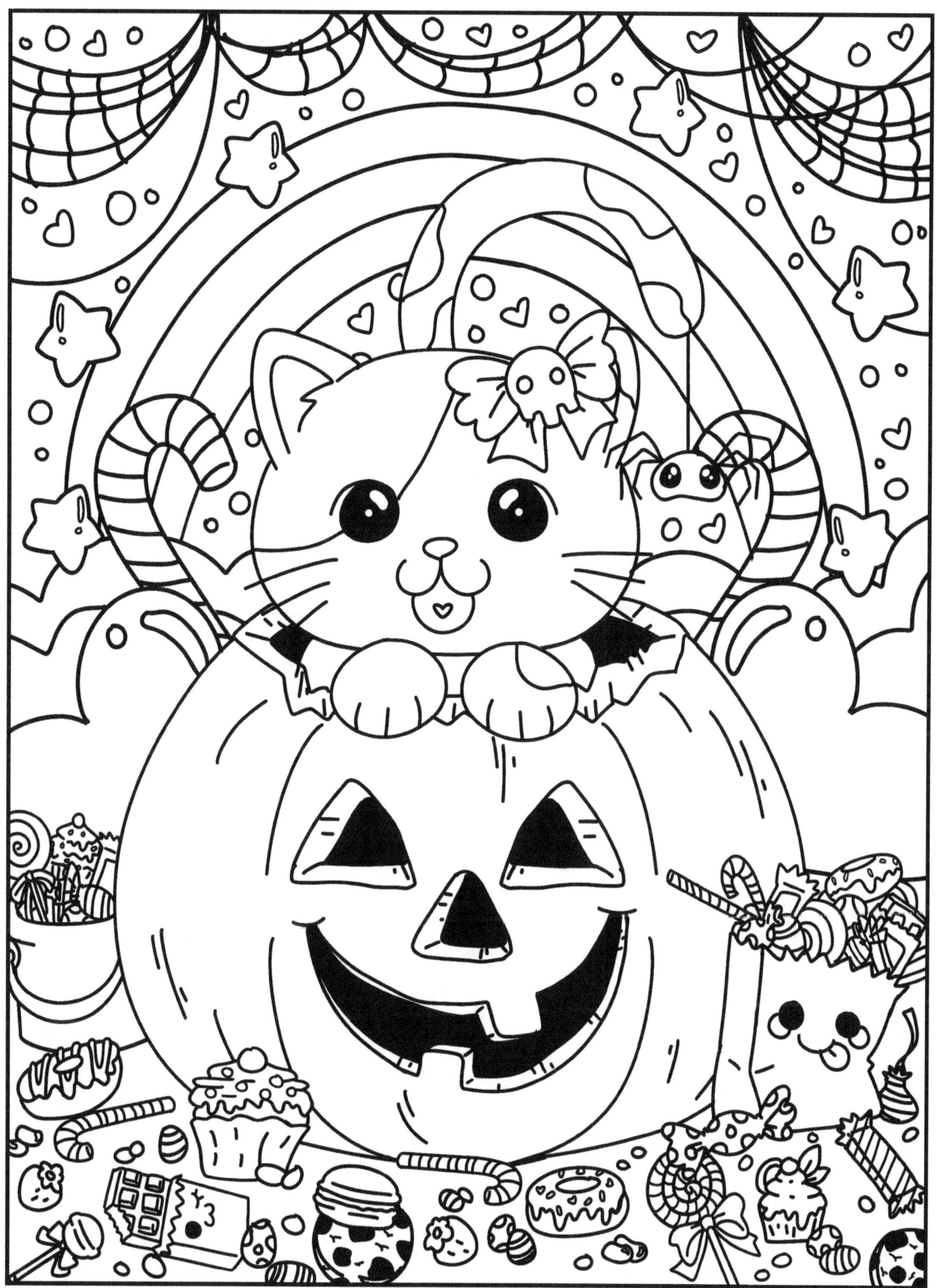

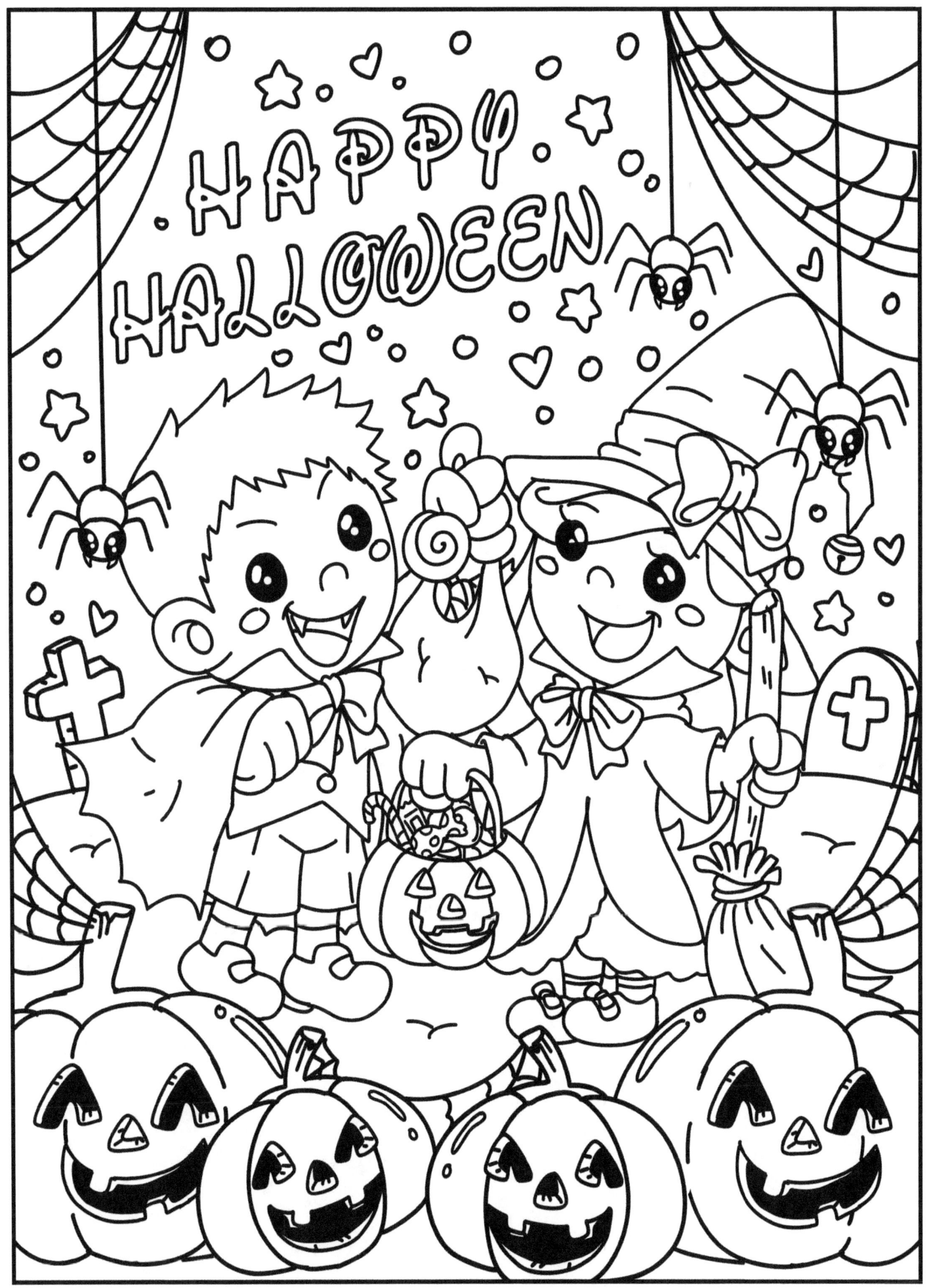

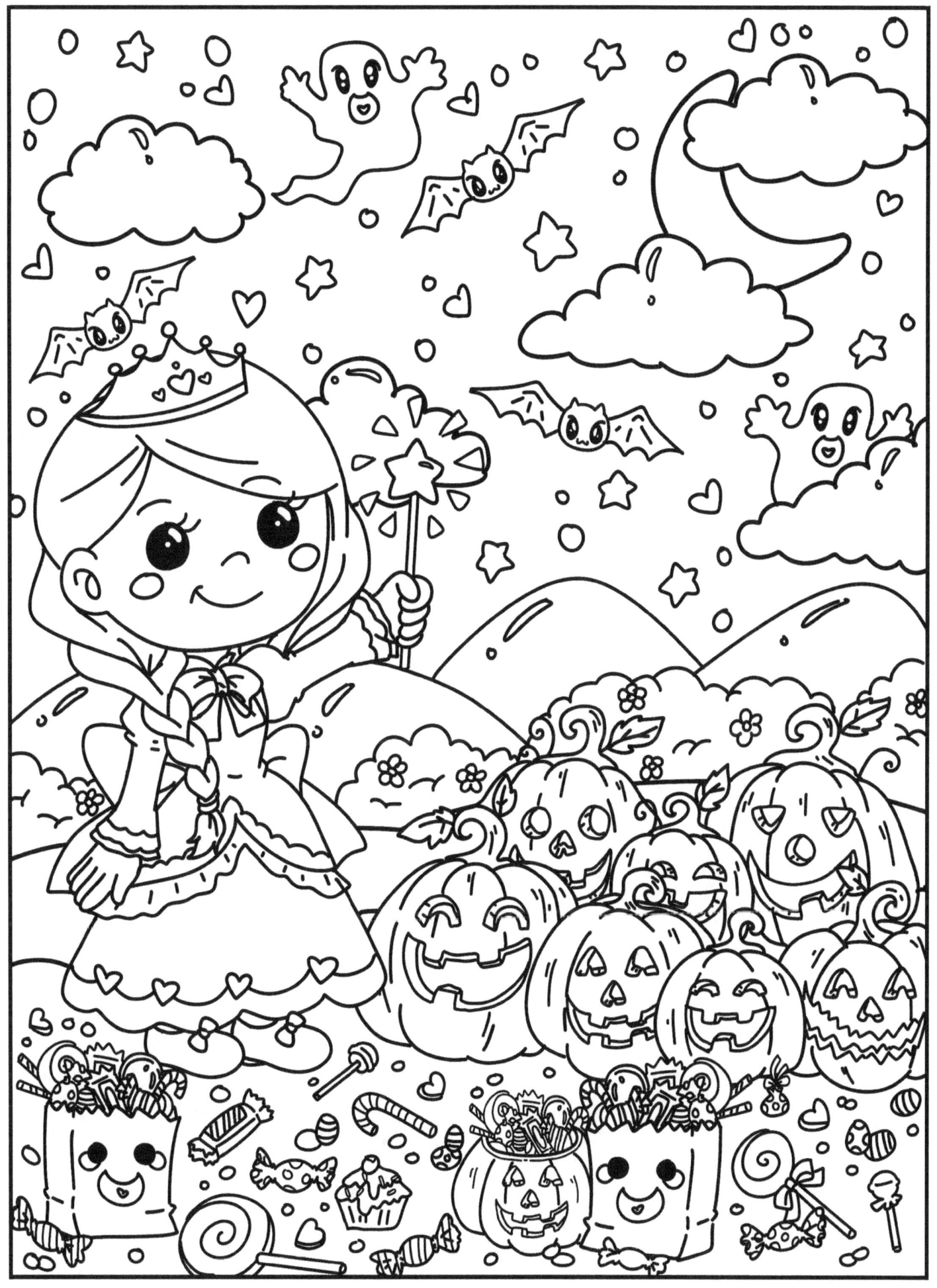

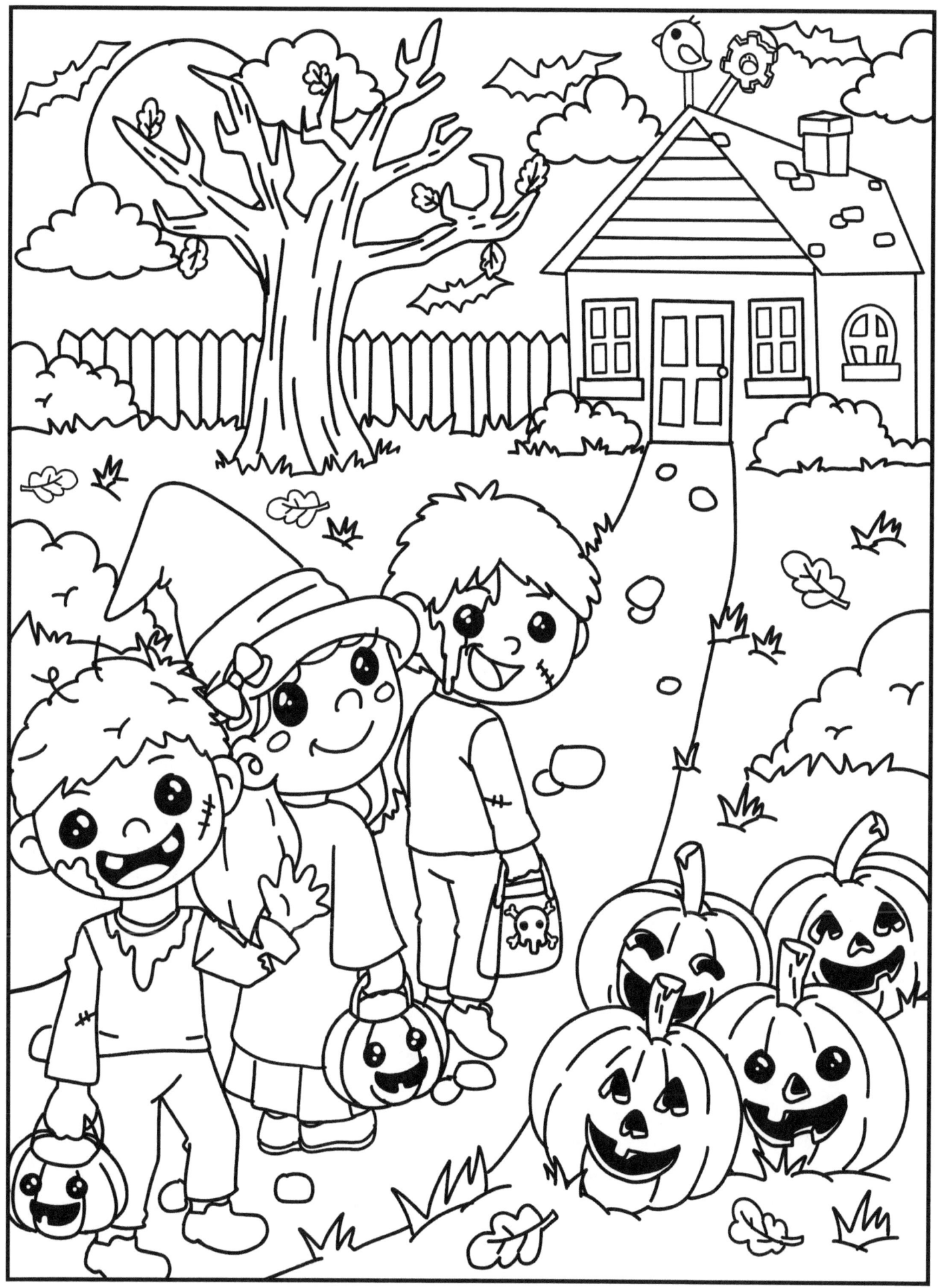

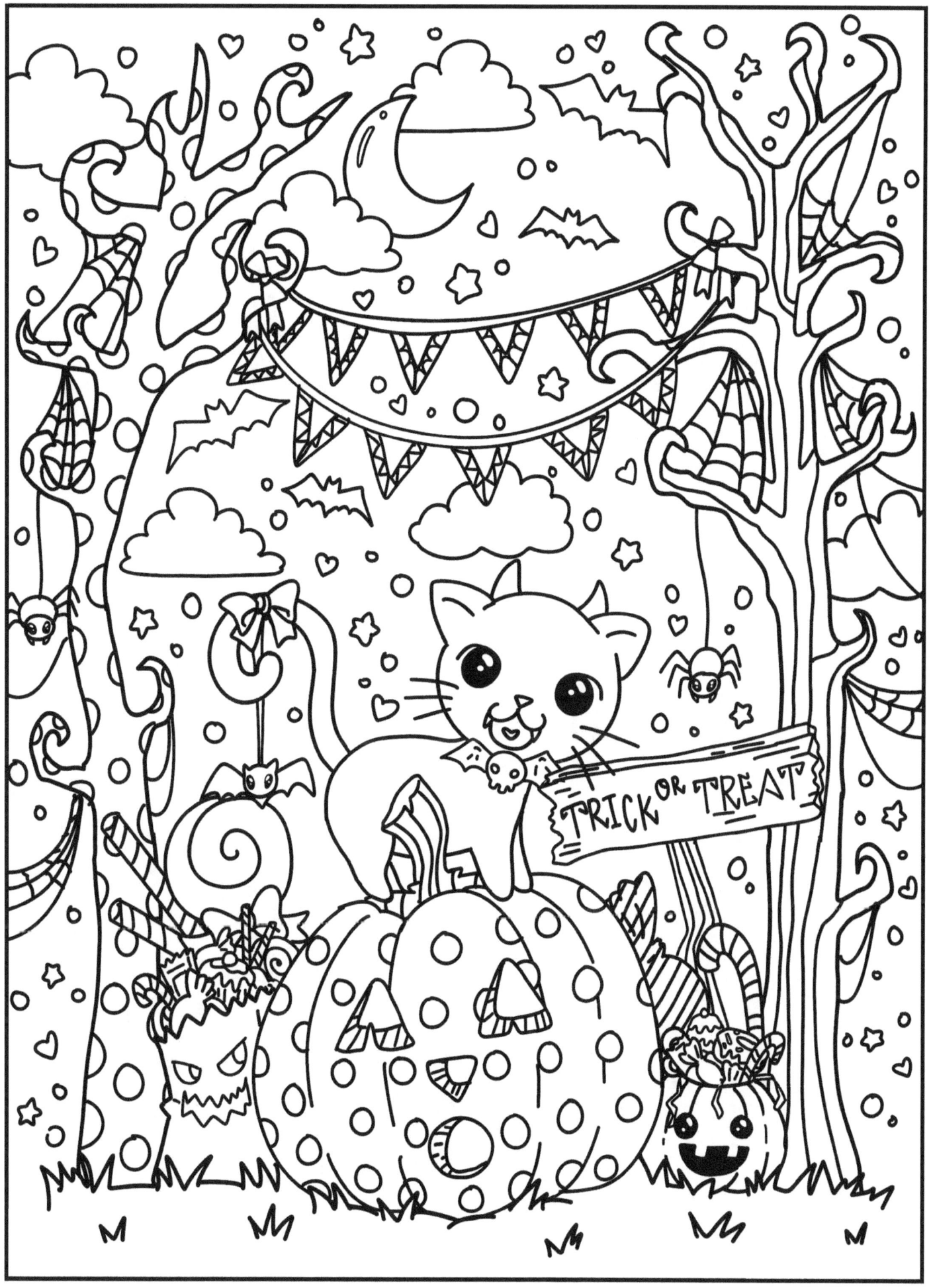

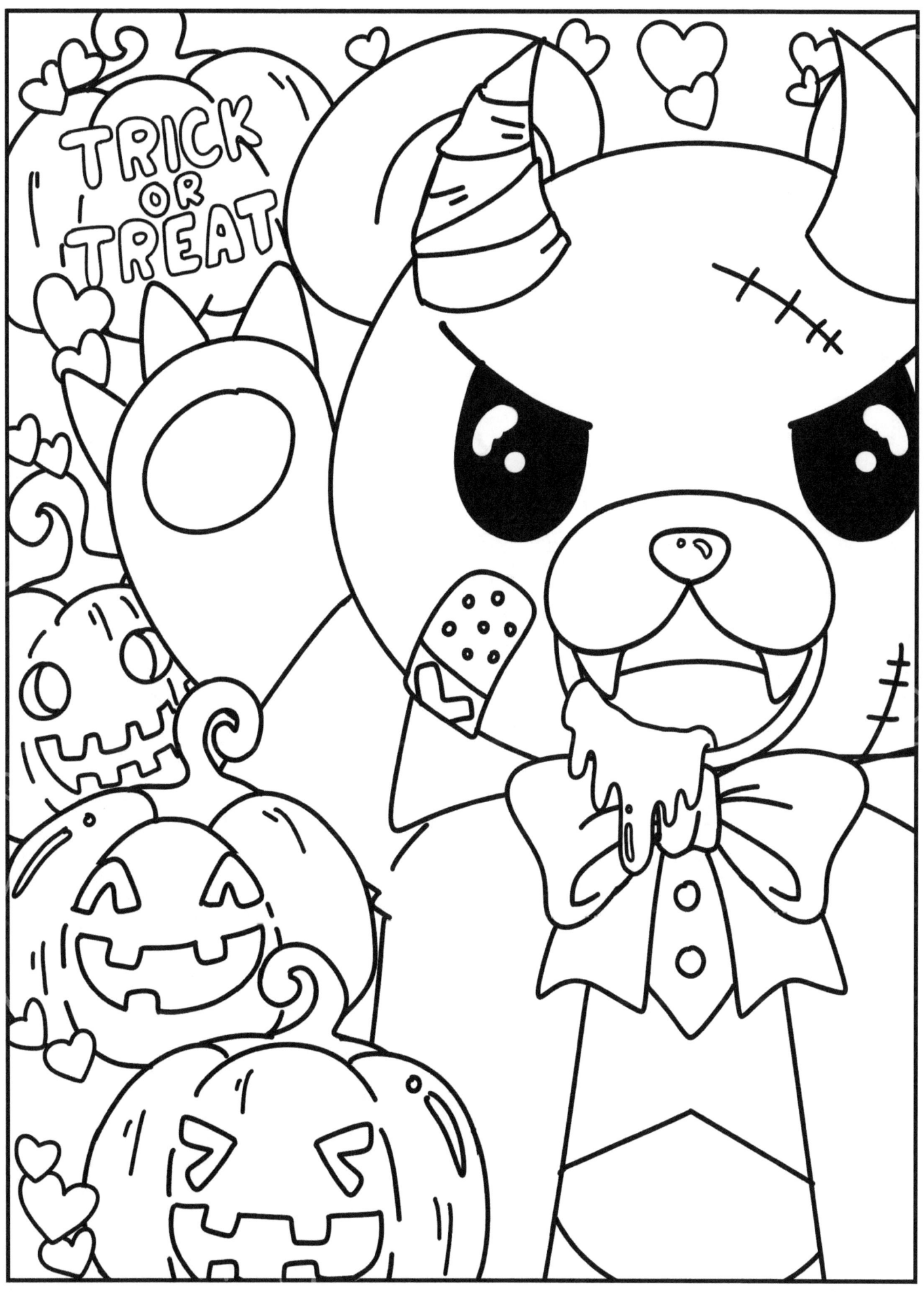

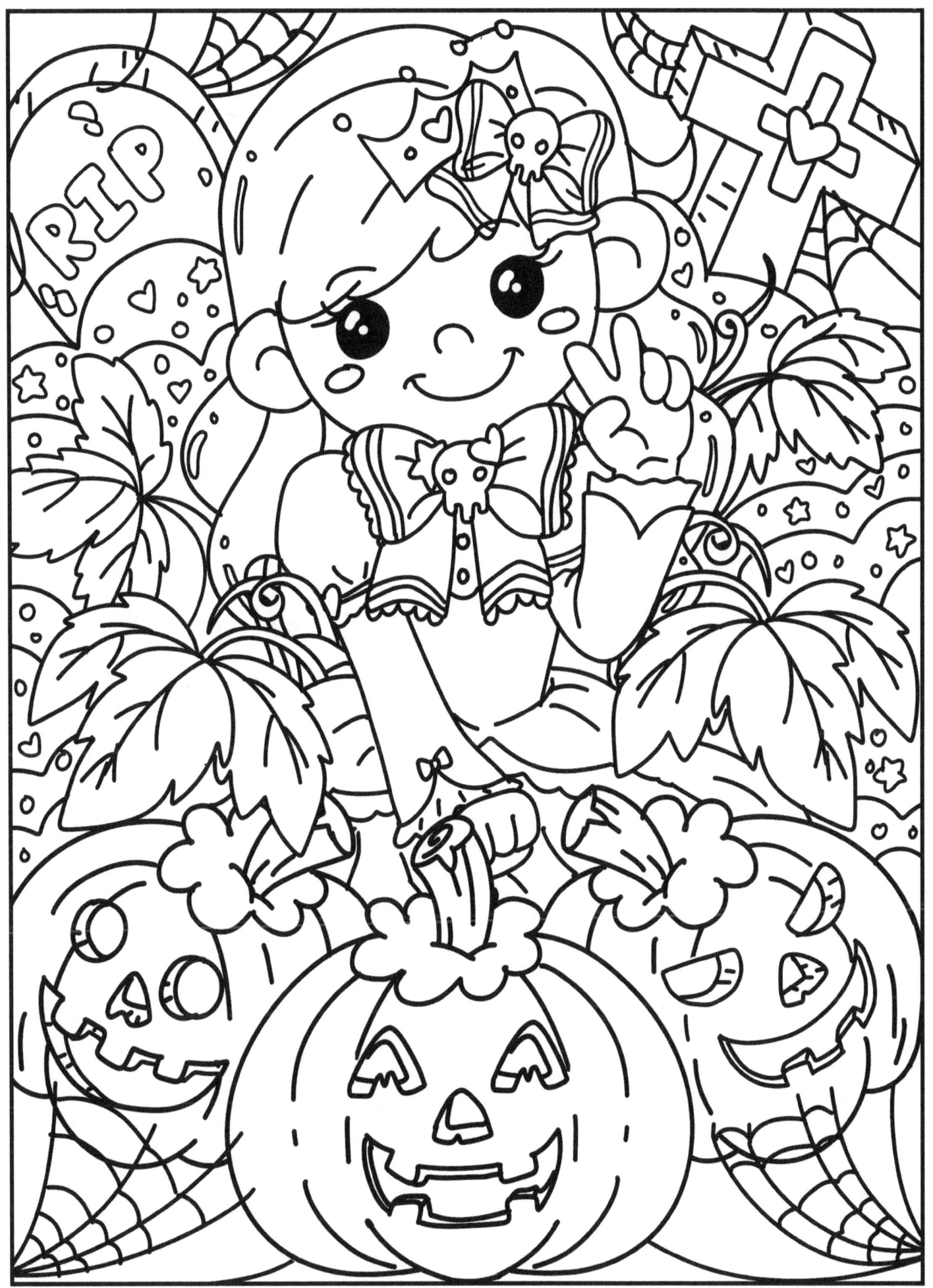

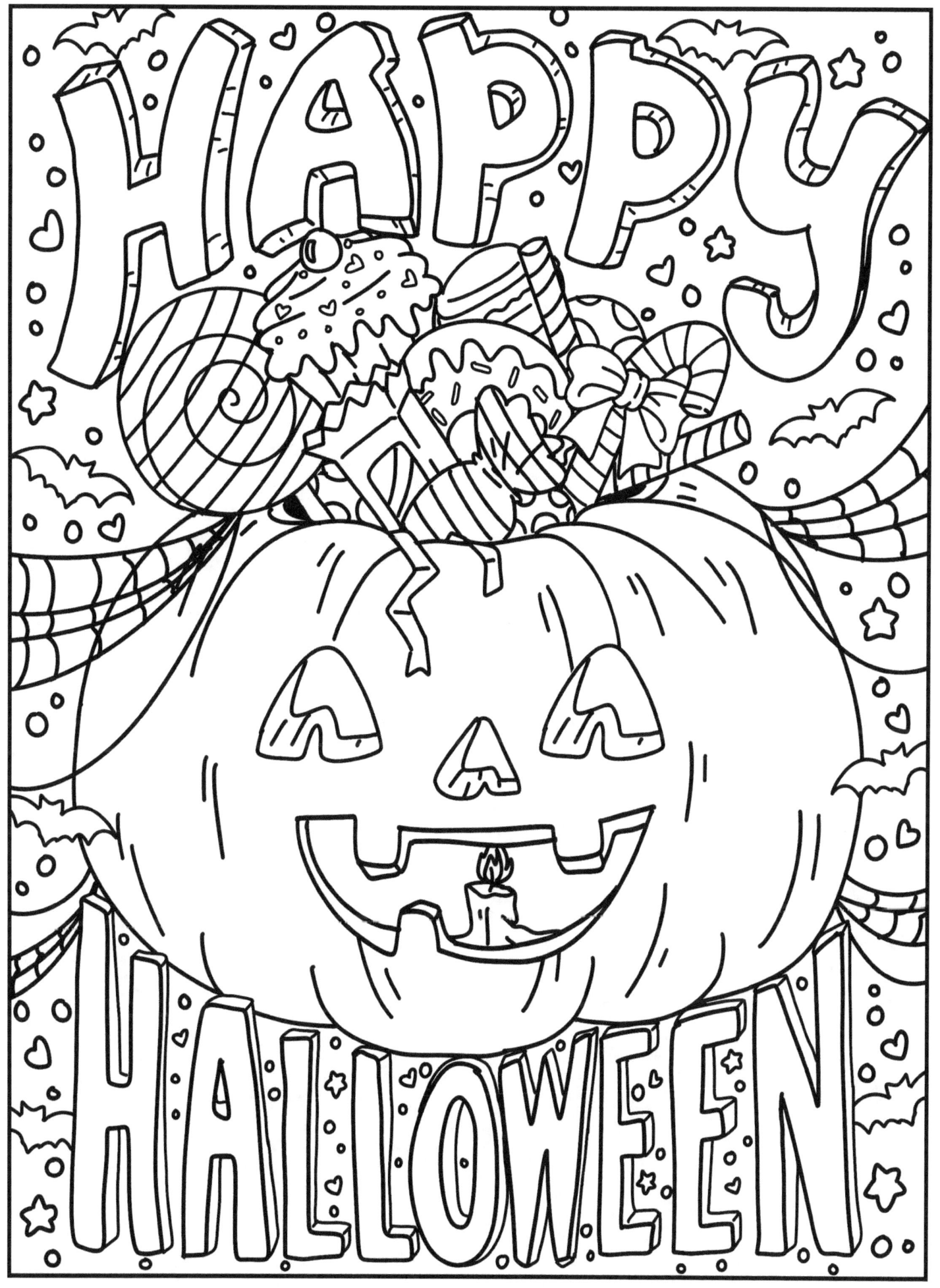

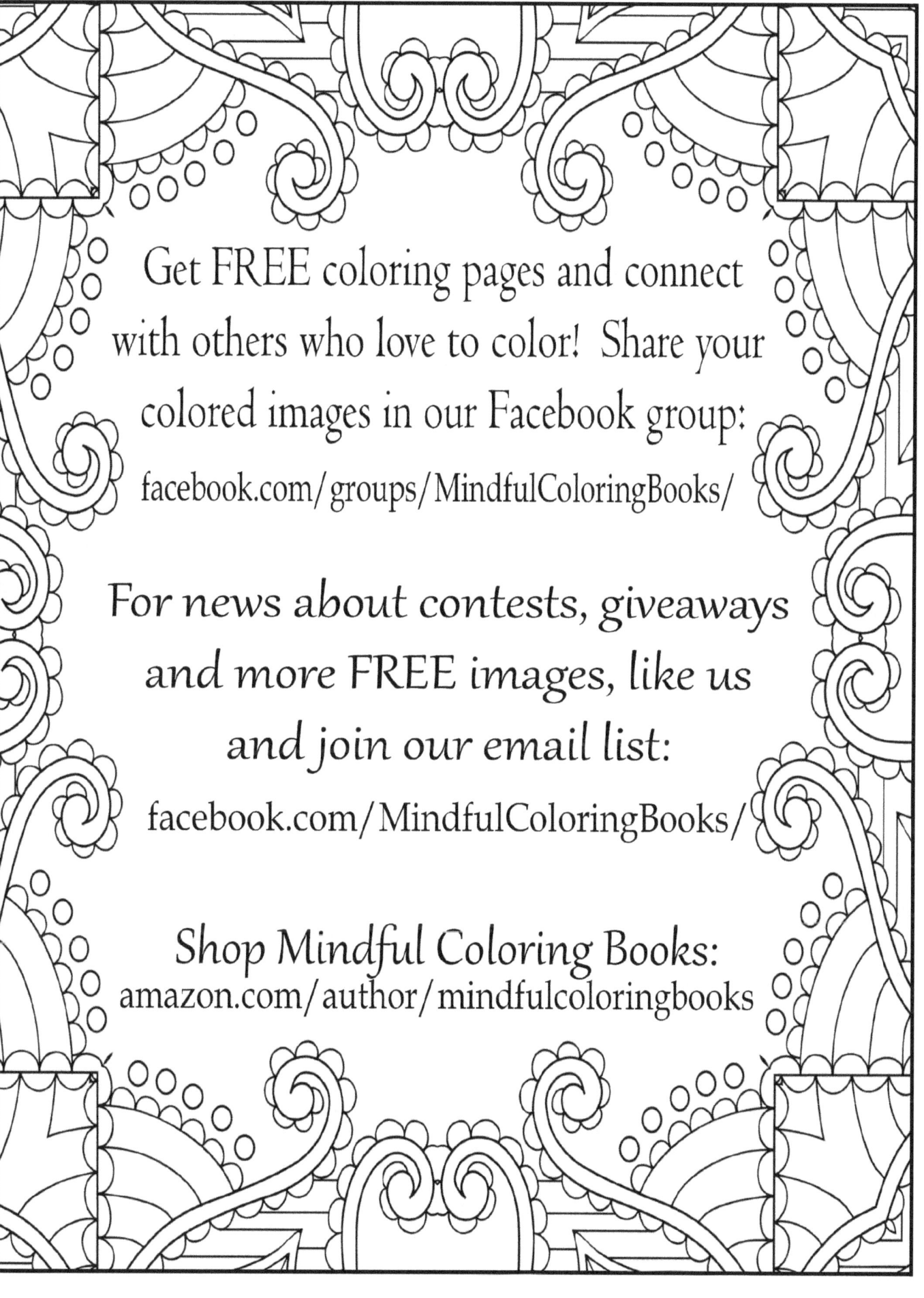

Get FREE coloring pages and connect with others who love to color! Share your colored images in our Facebook group: facebook.com/groups/MindfulColoringBooks/

For news about contests, giveaways and more FREE images, like us and join our email list: facebook.com/MindfulColoringBooks/

Shop Mindful Coloring Books: amazon.com/author/mindfulcoloringbooks

Enjoy these preview pages from
some of our other
coloring books!

Kawaii

Unicorns

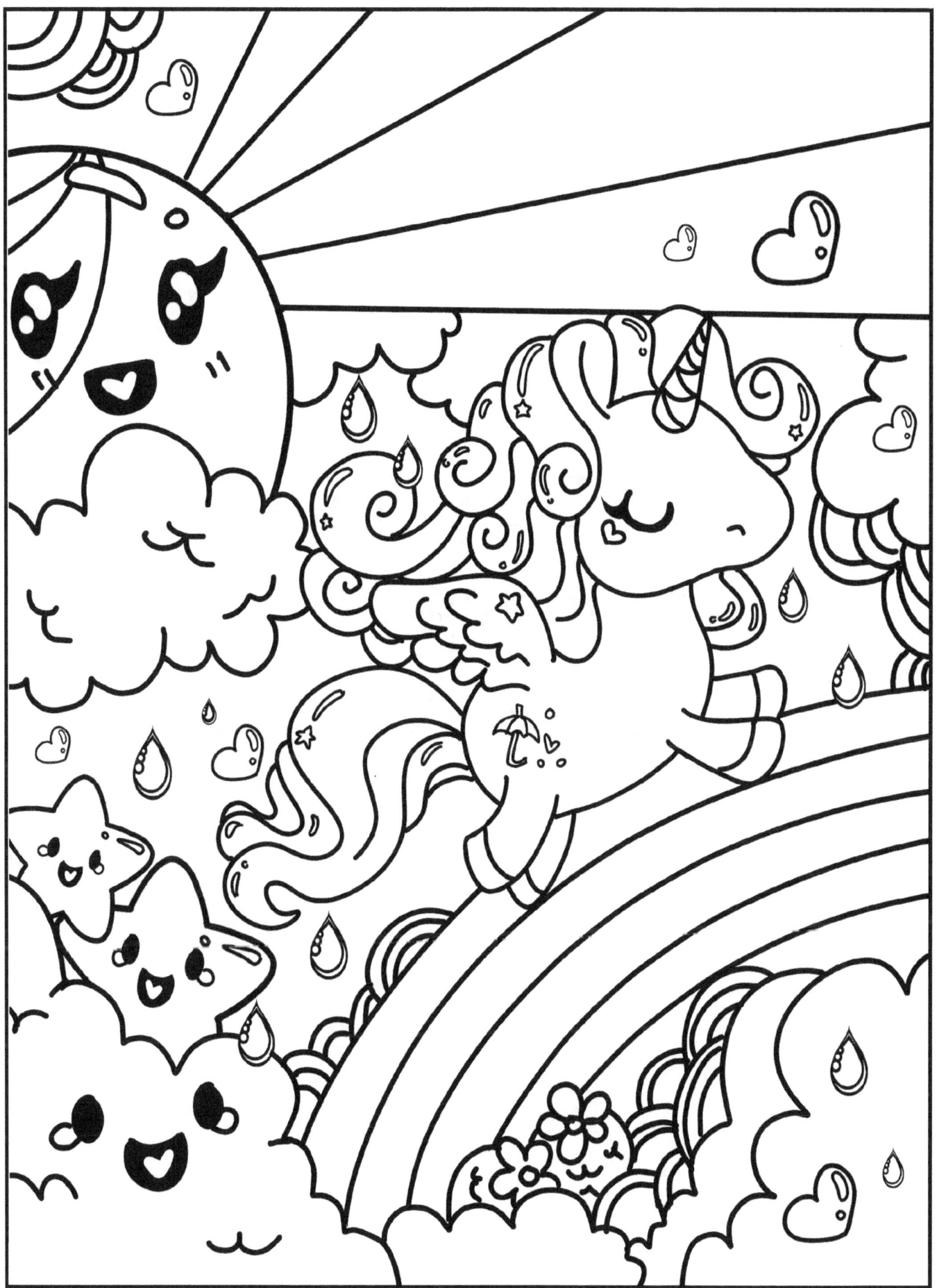

Cute Baby Animals
Coloring Book

Relaxing Coloring Book for All Ages

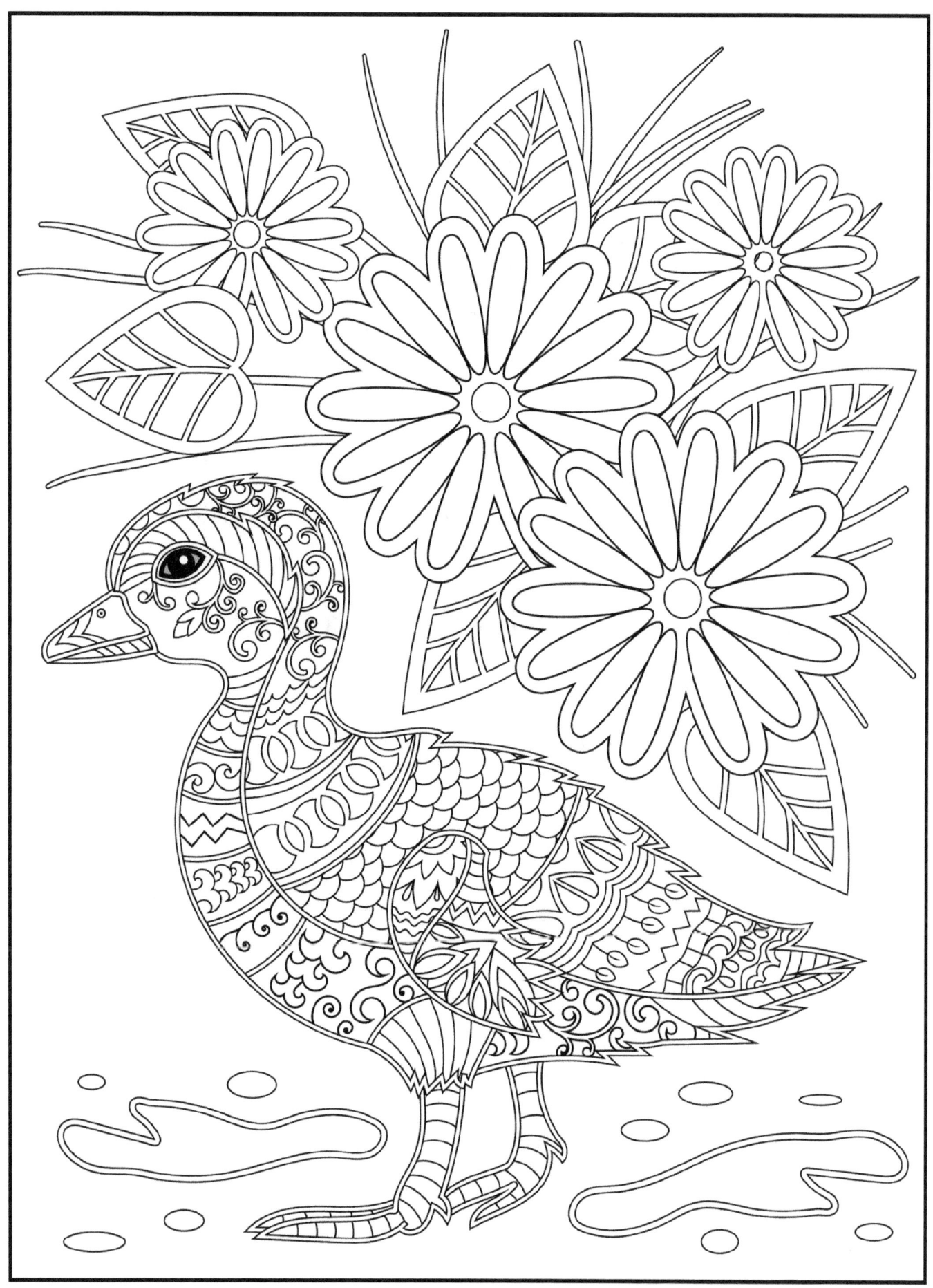

Color My Curls

Coloring book for adults

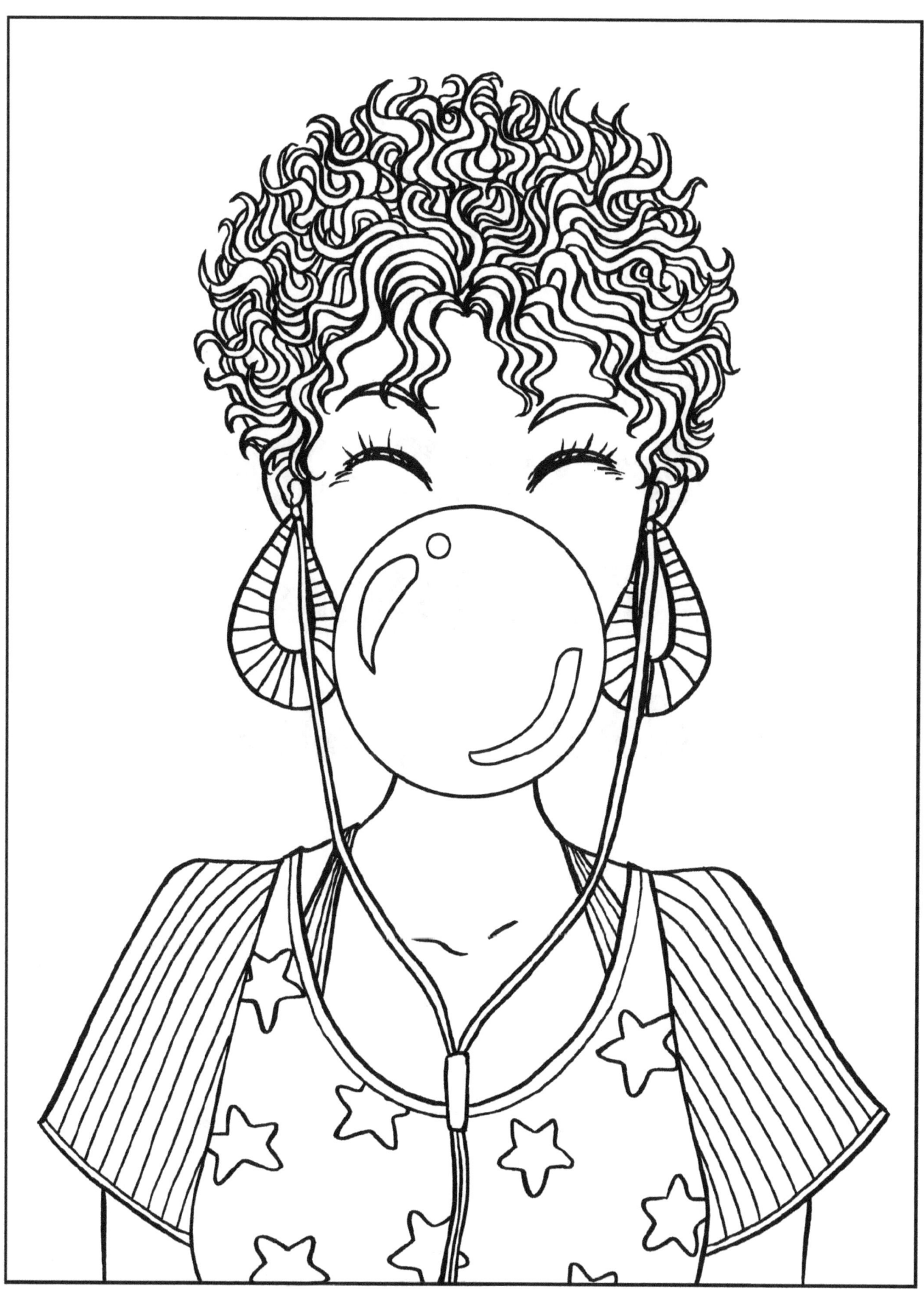

Kawaii Girl Fashion Coloring Book

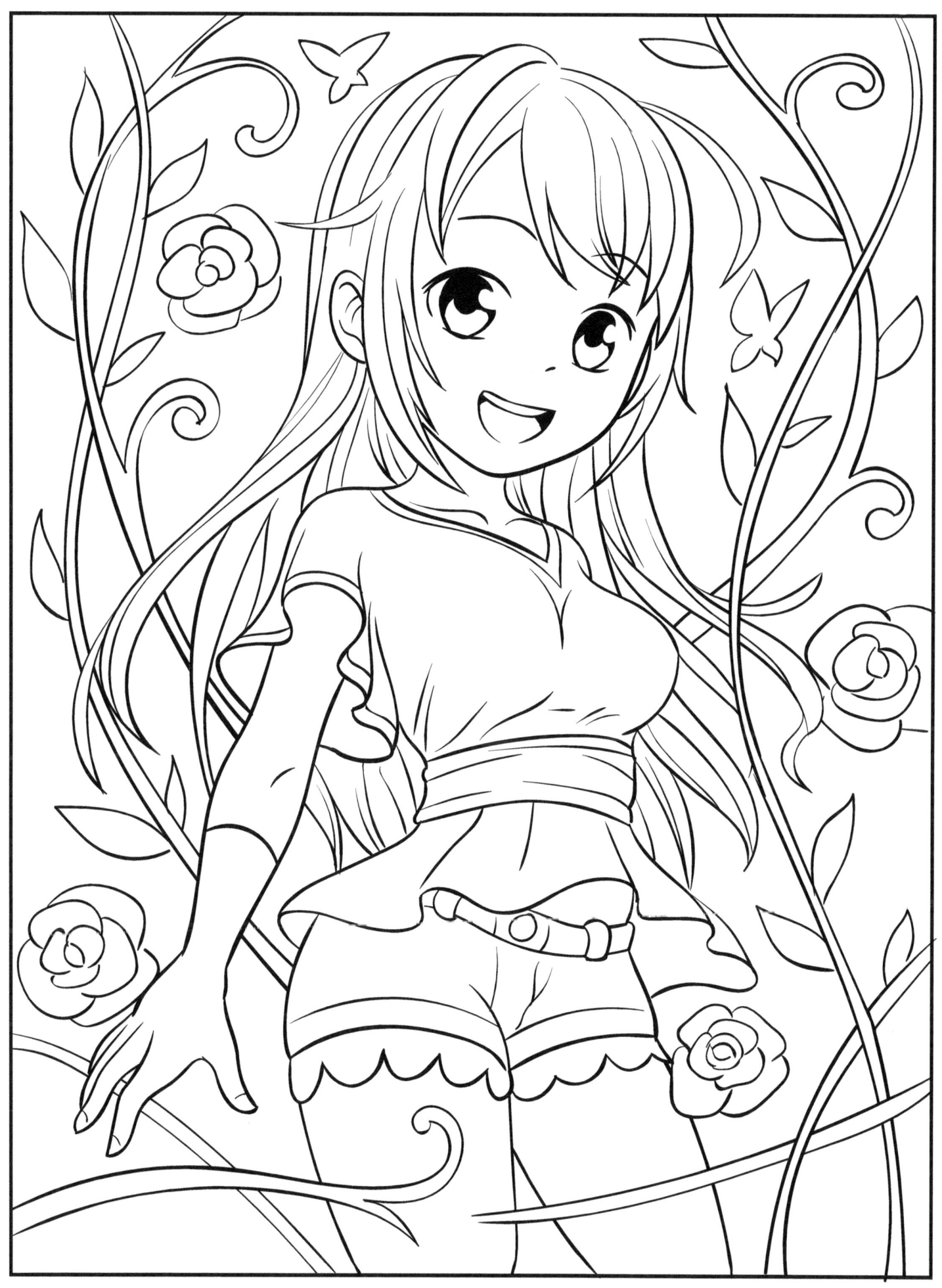

Free Bonus Stuff!

Color, cut out and share with your friends!

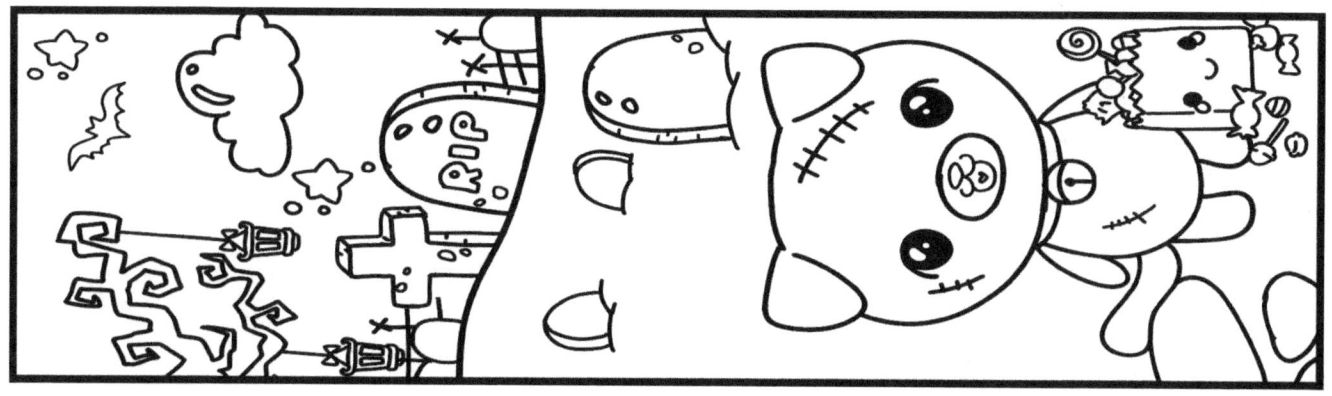

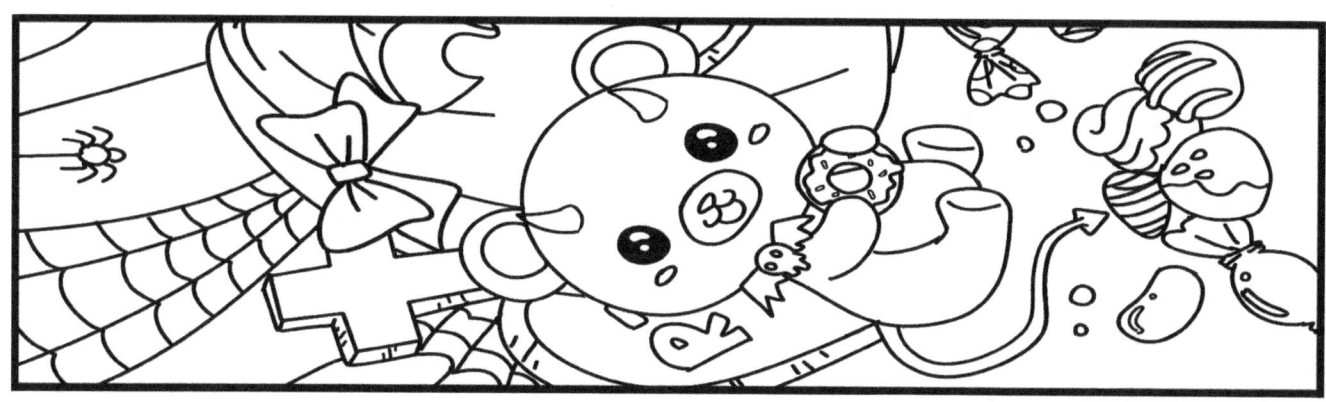

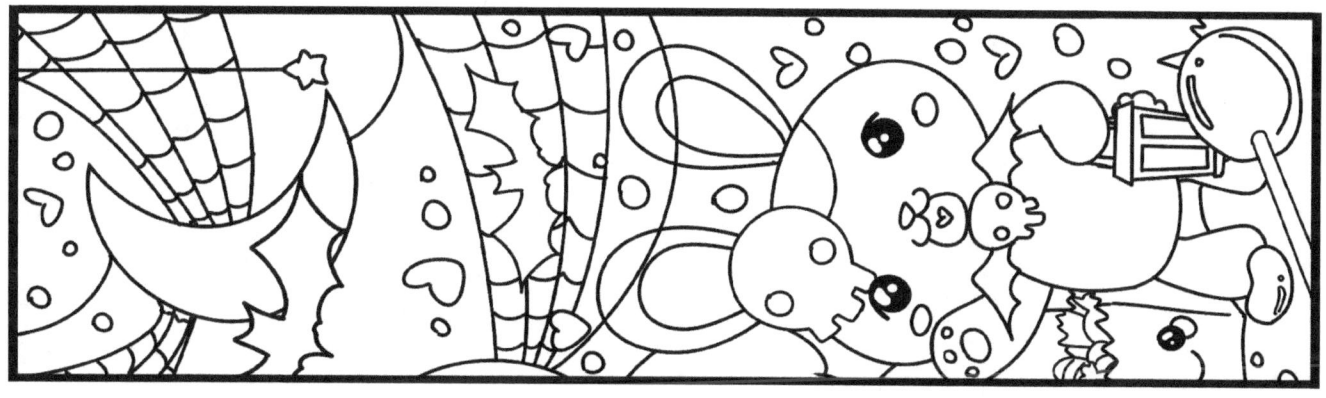

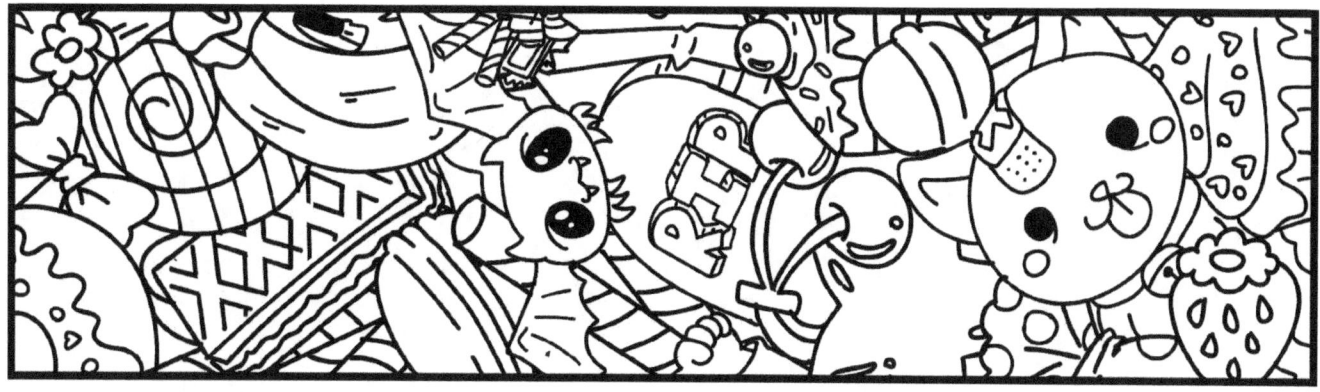

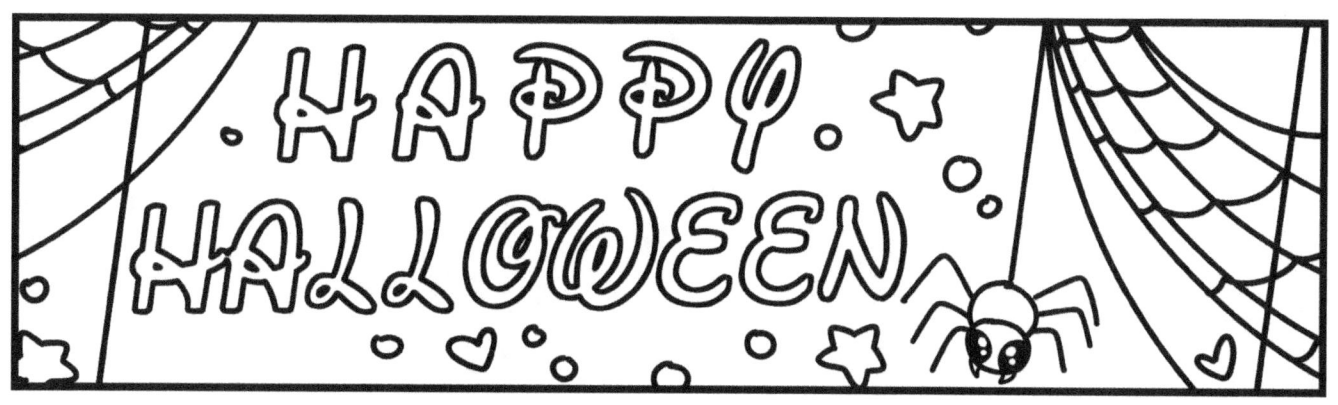

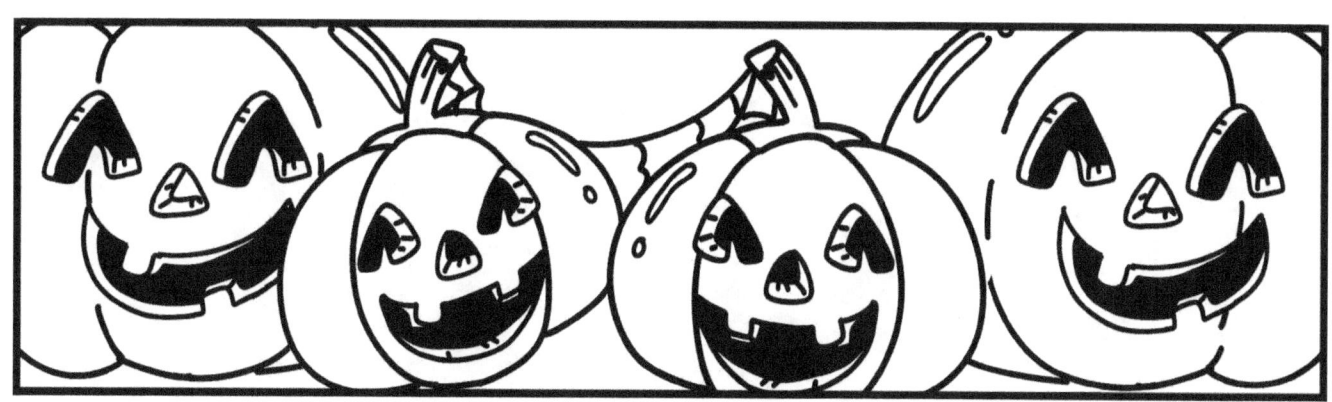

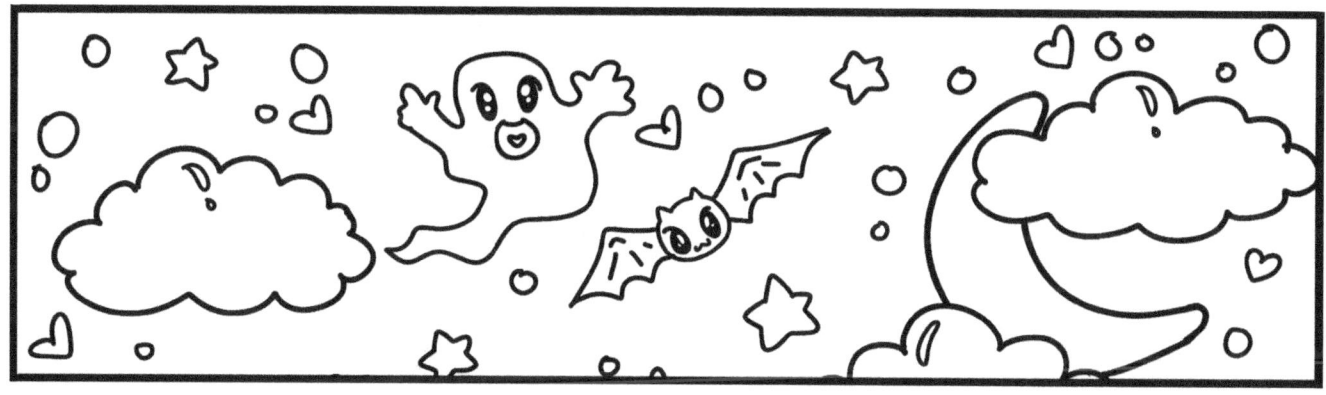

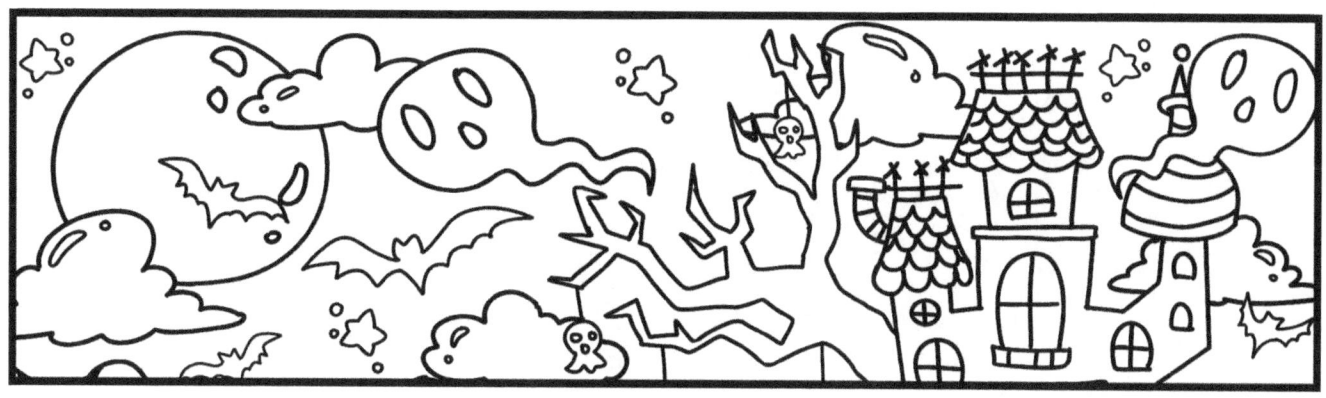